A Rose for Nana

& Other Touches from an Everyday God

*A Collection of Writings
by Carol Greenwood*

Aglow Publications

A Ministry of Women's Aglow Fellowship, Int'l.
P.O. Box 1548 • Lynnwood, WA 98046-1548
USA

Design and illustrations by Martine Fabrizio,
Technigraphic Systems, Inc. • Edmonds, Washington

Women's Aglow Fellowship, International is a non-
denominational organization of Christian women. Our mission
is to provide support, education, training and ministry oppor-
tunities to help women worldwide discover their true identity
in Jesus Christ through the power of the Holy Spirit.

Aglow Publications is the publishing ministry of Women's
Aglow Fellowship, International. Our publications are used to
help women find a personal relationship with Jesus Christ, to
enhance growth in their Christian experience, and help them
recognize their roles and relationship according to scripture.

For more information about Women's Aglow Fellowship,
please write to Women's Aglow Fellowship International,
P.O. Box 1548, Lynnwood, WA 98046-1548, U.S.A. or call (206)
775-7282.

Unless otherwise noted, all scripture quotations in this
publication are from the Holy Bible, New International Ver-
sion. Copyright 1973, 1978, 1984, International Bible Society.
Other versions are abbreviated as follows: TLB (The Living
Bible), Beck (The New Testament in the Language of Today),
KJV (King James Version).

ISBN 0-932305-87-3

*To my mother and to my husband and best friend, Dick,
and our children: Anne and her husband Alan;
Gail; Paul and his wife Ginny;
and Jane*

Table of Contents

Foreword

Dirty dishes. Runny noses. Spilled milk. Scattered newspapers. Friends who forget our birthdays. Children who quarrel. Death of loved ones. The tattered fabric of an everyday life. It's tedium ad nauseam unless you are looking for something else.

But for those who are, like our creative author Carol Greenwood, the garment of life is filled with pockets of joy, moments of wonder, soarings of inspiration, and insights into God in the most everyday moments.

God didn't come to be shut up in a cathedral, he came to be like us; to walk in sorrow and joy, pain and peace, weariness and exuberance—just like you and I do every day. He came to understand us, and because he does, he is found in the most mundane warp and woof of life. So put your hand deep in the folds of life to find the treasures hidden there.

Reading this book will awaken you to the nearness of a Father God who understands. Who cares. Who encourages his tired, discouraged children. You will come away from this book knowing, in a fresh new way, God's unconditional love for each of us.

You will want to share this book with all those

you love, because you will want them, too, to experience a newness of understanding of the God who walks beside us every day.

Joyful reading to you!
— Gwen Weising

Preface

For a few heart-stopping moments yesterday I thought I'd lost our granddaughter. It just happened that Andrea's two-week stay with Dick and me has coincided with the deadline for this book. Between editing and retyping, I've been having tea on the floor with Andrea and her dolls. Plus doing "Head and Shoulder, Knees and Toes" and the other twenty nursery rhymes on her cassette tape—every morning.

Yesterday she and I had a lot to do. I had to get the final corrections to the typist, and Andrea had to do her usual—explore the world. But her timing was bad, and she nearly gave me cardiac arrest.

I was upstairs, half-way through putting on my makeup when the silence downstairs registered an alert in my granny alarm. *Where is Andrea? It's too quiet down there.*

I raced downstairs, tore through every room in the house—twice—with no sign of her little towhead bobbing along. Into the laundry room where the large cat door loomed as a possible escape hatch for an exploring two-year-old. Outside in a flash, I ran through the yard shouting her name. No Andrea. To the front of the house and out in the street. I eyeballed the school playground to see if she could have wandered there. But she was nowhere in sight. Back in the house, heart pounding and frantic, I did one more speed pass through each room. Nothing. Outside again, tearing through the same route and up the street. Time to call for help—the neighbors first. Then 911.

I threw open the front door and there, quietly climbing the stairs, was Andrea, humming softly as she pushed a silver car across each step.

I don't know where she was or how I missed her. She'd probably ducked behind a door or a big chair. All I cared about was finding her and telling her how much I loved her. The lost was found. It was the best news I had all day.

The Encourager Column in *Aglow* magazine began eight years ago to convey that same message: that we have a Father who is not put off by our lostness. Instead, he has come close to find us. The same creator God who fashioned the universe, made majestic mountains, and painted awesome sunsets is also close at hand. He is not a "once-upon-a-time" God swooping down for a quick rescue and then leaving us to stagger through life alone.

The Gospel, the really Good News, is that God is here. Close. Forgiving. Teaching. Freeing. Loving. Comforting. Disciplining. Encouraging.

I hope this collection of the Encourager columns will encourage you to know that kind of a God even better. I hope that in telling simple, everyday stories in *A Rose for Nana* you, too, will encounter Jesus, the Hound of Heaven. He's looking to express his Father's love, right where you live.

My family urged me to put this book together. I'm grateful beyond words for their love, their support, their critiques, and their willingness to be exposed as human in our family stories. And for loading the dishwasher while I wrote! I am also deeply grateful for friends who cheered me on and for Kim Jamieson who has the fastest typing fingers in the West—and has done it all with incredible grace and cheerfulness.

Carol Greenwood
Seattle, 1990

A Touch of Forgiveness

Jesus said, "Father, forgive them, for they do not know what they are doing."
Luke 23:34

A Rose for Nana

uy her flowers—today. The nudge hit me five paces past the flower shop.

Great idea. I'll dash in on my way back from the park, I told myself, wanting to maintain stride and not lose the aerobic benefits of my walk. "I'll bring Nana a pink rose bud with some baby breath."

Nana, as we called my eighty-one-year-old mother-in-law, loved flowers. And before Dad died and she moved to an apartment, she gardened like crazy. In recent years, however, her innate Scandinavian thrift joined forces with her Depression mentality, and she rarely allowed herself the luxury of fresh cut flowers. In fact, whenever we crossed the state to visit her, she invariably reminded us not to bring her anything—especially flowers.

"They cost too much, and they just die anyway. Besides," she explained, "you and Dick need the money for the kids' education."

Eventually, I stopped arguing and resigned myself to arriving empty-handed at her doorstep.

But the issue with Nana went deeper than "no flowers, please." I'd struggled with her bluntness for years, ever since Dick and I swung by his parents' place on the way home from our honeymoon, and she volunteered to critique our wedding.

unny part was I liked her so well before ᵥᵥₑ were married. But in time, her no-nonsense nature and my tender Welsh bones collided. And kept colliding.

I couldn't shine floors like she could; I let weeds grow along the fence; we had too many cats; kids too close together; and I'd committed the unspoken crime of marrying her only child. I personalized it all, denied and buried the hurt, and emotionally distanced myself from her for thirty years.

Every so often, I'd ask the Lord to mend the relationship. I'd mentally hoist the white flag and wave the olive branch her way—all overtures that, from my perspective, were flatly ignored. I compared myself to a swimmer diving into icy water and repeatedly crawling toward shore, near death with hypothermia. Even Dick couldn't grasp my struggle, and his best efforts of consolation, "Ah, that's just Mom," never satisfied my expectation nor salved the open wound.

Finally, I decided I'd used up my "risk quota." My relationship with Nana stalemated at politeness, formality, even comfort from time to time, but never openness.

Just before this last trip to see Nana, the old wound surfaced again as unresolved things do. I inadvertantly spilled my need for help with a relationship during prayer request time at a women's Bible study. "I feel like I've turned myself inside out to extend forgiveness to someone, and a hook is still in me. I cannot get free of it," I told them.

The leader patiently drew me out. "Can you tell

us how you felt when this person first hurt you?"

The accumulated "stuff" in my gunny sack of hurts emptied out in front of caring, supportive, confidential women. Then came the surgeon's probe: "Carol, do you suppose you became defensive when you felt attacked?"

"Defensive? Of course." Without thinking, I spoke the self-incriminating words: "But I was right."

The diagnosis continued. "By holding on to your rightness, you've blocked the forgiveness you want. Would you be willing to lay your rightness down?"

Would I? Jesus had patiently waited me out. I'd taken a long ride—through Frustration Corner, past Hurting Junction, to the end of the line at Desperation City. I was ready for healing. More than ready. So was Jesus. Supernaturally, he exchanged my repentance for his peace. He could have dismantled the wall I'd erected between Nana and me with a celestial jackhammer, but instead he did it invisibly, quietly in my heart. But he did it. And I knew it.

Nana liked the pink rose I gave her when I returned from my walk. "Oh, for me? You shouldn't have done it, but you know, I haven't had flowers for years." She fussed with the baby breath until she was satisfied and moved the bud vase from the desk to the kitchen table and then back. Then she, who never initiated a hug and stiffened when others did, risked hugging me as Dick and I said our good-byes. Her parting words were "Thanks again for the flowers."

Two weeks later, we made another trip across the mountains—a painful trip. After a massive heart attack, Nana had quietly exited this world and entered into her eternal rest.

The florist quizzed me when I ordered flowers for the memorial service and a spray for the casket.

"Weren't you here a couple of weeks ago? You were so eager to get just the right rose for your elderly mother-in-law. I remember thinking how lucky she was to get it while she was still alive. Sometimes little fusses crop up in families, and our pride stops us from telling them we love them. If we wait too long, they die not knowing we care."

I nodded. "That can happen."

"But not your mother-in-law. That little lady knew you loved her."

"Yeah, she did," I said. She knew.

Loving an Old Friend

Alocal newspaper columnist recently described a beautiful reconciliation he and his wife had with an old friend.

His wife, Margaret, was ill with cancer, and together they agreed to pursue getting back with a dear old friend. The separation spanned fourteen years, and Margaret, tired of the hard feelings, wanted to see the friendship mended.

The wrench in their relationship hadn't come overnight. Margaret had literally grown up with her friend, and Larry had met her in his early twenties and for many years they both enjoyed a warm and deep friendship with her. A point came in their relationship, however, when things began to change. The old friend seemed to be headed in a different direction; communication became awkward and strained. Worse than that, they felt she was too bossy and judgmental about others. The differences finally became irresolvable, and the relationship ruptured. They could not continue to be together; yet they'd been friends for a long time, and it hurt to be separated.

Larry described their disappointment: "Frankly, I was angry," he admitted. "My feelings simmered along, undealt with through the years, finally degenerating into bitterness. I felt like I'd been blatantly betrayed." Although time gradually eased the intensity of their feelings, they continued the estrangement.

Wrestling with cancer, however, raised all sorts of new issues—including the lengthy alienation from their friend. The time had come, they decided, to reach out to her in peace. Mutual friends brought them up to date on what she'd been doing over the past years. As they listened, Larry and Margaret found themselves not only curious, but less critical and more understanding and compassionate about her human failings.

Finally, they decided to meet again. The surprise was that she extended herself to them immediately. They felt it when they walked in the door. She offered them forgiveness and love. She even gave them bread and wine, and they gratefully took it from her. A reconciliation had been effected; they were ecstatic to be back with their old friend, *the Church.*

The story reaches me. It stirs recollections of my own joys and frustrations over the years in relationship with the Church. Do you remember them? Those times growing up when you heard your first stories about Jesus from the lips of a dedicated Sunday school teacher. When you sat in rows and learned Bible verses and stood to sing "Jesus Loves Me." Maybe the Lord's presence first became real to you through the Word faithfully preached by a pastor. Or perhaps the example of an unpretentious saint, faithfully weeding the church flower beds imprinted the image of a servant's heart indelibly on your own.

The Church was a place where we felt at home; here we sensed the goodness of God, not only through the worship and teaching of the Scriptures, but also through the variety of God's people and their gifts as we rubbed shoulders with them Sunday after Sunday. As we laughed and cried with them.

Churches are filled with imperfect people, and that fact alone makes them sitting ducks for Satan's attacks. If they are making any impact for Christ and moving forward in the Gospel, they *will* have their ups and downs.

The apostle Paul knew these real-life struggles well and described them clearly in his letters to the early churches.

Things have not changed very much. We still have growing pains, personality conflicts, divisive issues, differences of opinions. Sometimes wrenching, splitting theological differences.

All of this can be terribly unsettling when we so count on the Church to be our refuge, our reliable spiritual home. How much we want to be comfortable! How much we expect. Perfection, at least. Excellent music, Spirit-led preaching, classes that stimulate our minds and stretch our faith, and people who accept and love us as we are. Certainly we need high expectations; we need a place to be fed and to grow spiritually, but we're naive if we expect "the perfect church"—one that will meet all our needs, all the time. That's the Lord's job!

That's why Larry and Margaret's story touched

me. In the face of their own disillusionment, they became lonely, hungry, and, at the same time, sensitive to the struggles within the Church. They then dared to look inward at their own attitudes and judgments.

I can relate. Who hasn't experienced crushing disappointments and unrealistic expectations from the Church? The real question is: Are we willing to forgive?

Resentment and bitterness in the long run are only cop outs, fueled by Satan's applause. They have no place in our heart if we love and honor Jesus who *"loved the Church and gave himself up for her...to present her to himself as a radiant church, without stain or wrinkle...but holy and blameless"* (Eph. 5:25-27).

God has chosen to work through his people, which includes local churches, to bless the whole world through their witness of his redeeming love. Criticism is the easy course—that and running away mad. But we have another option: to be the Lord's agents of reconciliation, to pray for our churches and our pastors, to be open, forgiving, committed to strengthening our relationship with our friend, the Church.

CHAPTER TWO

A Touch of Love

We love because he first loved us.
1 John 4:19

Love Letters

*W*hen my dad died twelve years ago, he left me a few mementos: his pilot's compass, a college banner, assorted snapshots, and his engineering slide rule. That was it in the way of a tangible inheritance. And that was okay. The absence of material gifts seemed to enhance the real treasure, the priceless and highly personal legacy—my memories of life with Dad.

No inherited souvenir could have been recycled, replayed, or reworked more. I've savored every memory a thousand times in these intervening years, the good ones and the painful ones. In mid-life, childhood memories satisfy that voracious drive to piece together the puzzle of who we are.

Like I said, the memories were enough. But then, a month ago, out of the blue, in a ratty old suitcase, something else came from my dad's "stuff." Something bundled up from his desk and sent along when my stepmother sold their home. Letters. A bundle of them, yellowed and stuffed into envelopes with archaic-looking stamps. Every letter I'd ever written to him was there, from the time I was seven years old until his death.

I will never again minimize the value of writing a personal letter. Or receiving one.

I settled at the kitchen table to read my bundle

of letters. Dick was working late at his office. The house was quiet. My tea was hot. An ideal setting for some reflective reading. Alone and still, the perfect time to be mentally jarred back to the forties. I expected to capture a new perspective of what it was like to grow up during World War II. Reading over my old letters, I assumed, would be like taking a benign cruise down memory lane. I never expected more.

"Dear Far-away Daddy, ple-e-ease try to come up for my birthday." The opener of that first tablet-lined letter grabbed me by the heart. From there on, I was undone, emotionally dynamited, shredded inside by the pathos of the lonely seven-year-old letter writer. The little girl, who happened to be me. "You don't have to bring a present, but could you bring my books, my paper dolls, and my teddy from our old house?"

Instant replay: my old toys leapt to life through those words. But the real gut wrencher was the closing line: "If you can't bring the stuff, ple-e-ease come anyway."

After the first three letters, my eyes were too wet to read. I stood up for a breather. And to careen around the room for a few minutes. I stepped on Felix the cat, dumped my cold tea for a box of Kleenex, and sat down for another "go" with the musty papers.

Nothing I've read recently has impacted me so strongly. Meager literary value, but priceless in helping the little girl inside come to terms with her childhood. Without these letters, I'd never have "seen" the path that led from "Dear Far-away Daddy..." to the high school version: "Dear Dad, I'm editor of the yearbook now. I can't imagine why they chose me. Desperate, I guess. It'd be neat if you could come up, but I suppose you're pretty busy."

Needless to say, this exposure brought a tremendous healing perspective for old wounds, deeper acceptance of parental failures, and, ultimately, authentic forgiveness. And I'm overwhelmed that my dad, with all his struggles, saved a stack of his kid's letters. That in itself was a strong message, a love letter back to me.

In our busy society, not many people write personal letters. At a recent writers conference, I challenged one group with the fact that not everyone will publish a novel, but we can all write letters. One woman wrote me to say that her fourteen years as a legal secretary taught her to prepare good business letters, but not to share herself. Now she was going to start writing personal letters.

Phone calls are so easy. We can instantly "reach out and touch someone" via the phone. I've thought lately, though, about the poverty of soul in a nation that someday might not have the enrichment of letters the caliber of those written by Robert E. Lee and Stonewall Jackson. These men chronicled their agony of leading soldiers in the bloody, divisive Civil War. They wrote of their devotion to God and families in long letters that continue to bring them and their time period to life.

I am glad the apostle Paul didn't have a telephone. I'm glad the believers in Corinth, in Colosse, and throughout the Middle East could be buoyed by reading his vulnerable expressions of love, by his challenge to stand firm in the faith, and by his admonitions to grow in grace. Where would the Christian Church be today without all his letters of encouragement and instruction?

I've saved few of the crafts our kids made. But, as far as I know, I've saved all their letters. One flittered out of an old book just last week: "Mom, hang in there, baby. You're doing okay."

Letters. We need to write them, and we need to receive them. Not only because they record history and add depth and richness to our lives, but because we desperately need them as vehicles to share the love of our heavenly Father.

Letters. I'm so glad my dad saved mine. More than that, I'm glad my heavenly Dad wrote me first, passionately telling me from Genesis to Revelation that he knows me and he cares. I need letters like that—love letters.

Circles in the Sand

*W*hat I was hearing was no run-of-the-mill backyard squabble. The usually congenial and even-tempered neighbor kids—a sister and brother team—were engaged in full-scale verbal warfare in their corner sandbox.

From my weed-pulling vantage across the street, I could hear and observe the whole scene.

"Stop it, Teddy. I want you out of here!" Five-year-old Rachel shrieked at brother Teddy, issuing an unequivocal directive. "You can't cross my line."

"Lemme in!" Teddy, three, was less sophisticated and his low voice more plaintive, but he was coming on strong in persistence. "I tell Mommy," he retaliated, at the same time slyly nudging one foot slowly across the Maginot Line drawn in the sand by Big Sister.

"I said, 'Out.' I don't want you here." Rachel's voice was louder and more emphatic. "Go play with your trucks somewhere else. You're too little, and you always wreck my stuff. I drew this circle to keep me in and you out."

You wouldn't call stocky little Teddy a push-over, but he was beginning to sound like someone who'd just been outflanked by age and cunning. "Me wants in, too," he yelled in desperation. In a last ditch maneuver, he threw himself bodily across the sacred boundary.

Teddy's action ended the cold war. Sparks ignited. Fists flew. Legs kicked. Both kids screamed, "Mommy!" at peak decibel level. Fortunately, for everyone, Mommy flew out of the house to quell the riot, close the sandbox for the afternoon, and dispense naps to her two tired warriors.

I went back to weeding, pausing long enough to notice that during my eavesdropping break I, too, had absentmindedly drawn in the dirt. In fact, I had etched a circle, one to keep the azaleas "in" and the Great Enemy crab grass "out." Though nothing more than a tidy botanical marking between the "good guys" and the "bad guys," I suddenly understood why Rachel had drawn her circle in the sand.

Drawing lines, it seems, is an easy way to distinguish the good from the bad, the desirable from the undesirable, the "in" group from the "out" group. On the surface, it seems like a convenient, natural technique to manage life and stay "in charge" in a world where it's a challenge to distinguish black, white, and gray. Draw a line, erect a barrier, make a distinction. Get things settled into categories. Once a line is drawn, our fears can be shoved aside, and the sentinels "Safe" and "Secure" can guard our lives, allowing us the freedom to rest in confidence because we're comfortably on the inside.

Jesus confronted this when he dealt with the teachers of the Law and the Pharisees, the group who persisted in using the Law to draw lines to prove who was "in" and who was "out."

Remember how they brought the woman caught in adultery to him? They waited with baited breath to see whether he could circumvent the Law of Moses and ignore her transgression or if he would find her guilty and encourage stoning.

As you recall, Jesus didn't immediately answer. Instead, he bent over and drew with his fingers on the ground. Could his doodling have been a circle? A circle would have perfectly illustrated what these Jewish leaders were trying to do—separate the sinner from the righteous ones by imposing the Law as their dividing line of judgment.

Jesus, however, wouldn't have it. Not then and not now. No law, not even the venerable Law of Moses, could be used to exclude someone from the Father's love and mercy. He silenced their self-righteous judging by challenging the sinless one in their midst to throw the first stone at the guilty woman. He refused to be hemmed in by tradition or the constraints of a written code. His Father's love was directed at freeing and restoring, not condemning. And this radical turnabout left them all speechless, unprepared for the triumph of mercy over judgment (see James 2:13).

I've had to count myself in with Rachel and the Pharisees more often than I like to think. Who knows how many times I've drawn lines or circles to protect myself or defend God's reputation? Yet at the time I never dreamed I was closing myself off from others or being self-righteous. I was simply acting out of "discernment" and "self-preservation." I quietly retreated, closing myself off and protecting my feelings.

However, I'm jolted awake from this pattern when I unexpectedly find myself in a situation where a circle has been drawn and I, like Teddy, am in the sandbox, on the outside looking in.

When that happens to us the message is clear: it hurts to be overlooked, excluded, and judged. It hurts—a lot. And the only road out for us is the same road Jesus took and the one he continually urges us on; the road that risks reaching back out in unconditional love.

"He drew a circle that shut me out—
Heretic, rebel, a thing to flout.
But Love and I had the wit to win,
We drew a circle that took him in."
                    - Edwin Markham

The Boys in the Locker Room

We did it on a dare. One afternoon after high school debate practice, three of us girls covered our head with our sweatshirts, removed our shoes, and set a watch for the janitor. When the coast was clear, we darted into the most forbidden, off-limits place in our teenage world—the boys' locker room.

To our surprise, this masculine inner sanctum wasn't that different from the girls' locker room. Perhaps the "fragrance" of sweaty tennis shoes hung heavier in the air and more dirty socks lay in the corners, but overall the rooms were almost identical.

Talk about a let down! We'd risked our necks to enter the bastion of high school maledom, where no female dared tread, only to discover the cement floor, metal lockers, and squared, frosted windows were just like ours across the hall.

Yet we knew an unseen difference separated these two places. The boys' locker room wasn't only where boys suited up for games, but also, according to our older brothers, the place where boys talked about, bragged about, exalted, or put down girls.

We decided such chauvinism deserved retribution. We would sneak in, find the invisible macho

35

mystique, grab it, and run, striking a mortal blow to this male fortress. But the place wouldn't yield to our schemes; we found it to be a big nothing. Disappointed, we slinked out empty-handed.

Except for those years when the odor of our son Paul's tennis shoes escaped under his bedroom door, the memory of the boys' locker room nearly faded. Until last week when my friend Janet rang me early in the morning.

"Carol," she blurted out, "the boys in the locker room are dead!"

"I didn't know they were sick," I quipped without thinking. Then, retracting my flippancy, I pursued, "Who's dead? What boys?"

"The boys in the locker room," she repeated. "Remember I told you how they've plagued my marriage? Every time Fred and I argue about my wanting verbal affirmation or affectionate words, he'd dig his heels in, get tight-lipped, and retreat into walled silence. When I pleaded to know why he refused to express his feelings, he always blamed the same culprits—the boys in the locker room."

I did remember. As a sensitive teenager, Fred reacted to the constant locker room bragging. He was sickened by the tales of flattery and romantic words used to con girls into dates or press them for physical intimacy. He hated the unrestrained adolescent bravado—the raucous laughter, innuendos, and dares. He vowed he'd *never* manipulate girls with words. No way was he going to tell a girl she was pretty or that he liked her just to get a kiss. Not him. He refused to be a hypocrite. He'd play it straight with girls.

Unfortunately, Fred's decision didn't dismiss the locker room boys from his life. His anger only sent them underground where, like ghosts, they haunted his marriage for twenty-five years. He loved his wife. He knew, at least in his head, she needed to hear loving words; but he couldn't say them. Meanwhile the phantoms faithfully replayed the old locker room scenes in his mind, cementing his tender heart. Afraid to be vulnerable, he retreated into himself while his wife grew frustrated, angry, and desperate.

Janet's story was familiar. I'd heard it all before: "same trees, different monkeys." I call it the common wail of many women: unexpressive, silent husbands and emotionally hurting wives.

However, Janet's voice breathed hope. I urged her on.

"Six months ago, I opened fire on God about my frustration with Fred. I dumped a lot of anger right out on the table where I was reading the Bible. I reminded him about Paul's admonition for husbands to love their wives. I asked him why I had to suffer because some boys in a locker room said dumb things about girls years ago."

"And did you get an answer?" I asked.

"Well, yes. When I stopped yelling, my eyes fell on Jesus' words in Matthew 22: *'Love the Lord your God with all your heart and with all your soul and with all your mind....Love your neighbor as yourselves'* (vv. 37-39). Familiar words, but this time they nailed me; they collided with my will and exposed my heart.

"All along I blamed Fred for being unexpressive, but now I saw another side. I saw idolatry—mine! Instead of depending on the Lord to fulfill my need to feel secure and significant, I'd groveled at the altar of affirmation, demanding Fred meet all my emotional needs. I'd made him God, and he was only human. No wonder he resisted."

And the boys in the locker room? Janet stopped fighting them. And stopped blaming Fred for failing her. She was too busy setting her heart on God's love and loving her husband with new openness and acceptance. And the miracle—what the Lord knew all along—was that his unconditional, limitless love would turn her demanding spirit inside out and satisfy her deepest longings.

Satisfy and overflow. The morning Janet phoned me, Fred had taken her by the shoulders, looked her straight in the eye, and said "Honey, this is long overdue. I love you with all my heart."

At that moment the ghosts of the locker-room boys keeled over. Dead. Slain by a Father whose love always conquers.

Two Little Words for Moms

*T*his one's for you moms. Or, if you're English, "mums." Daughters, listen up; you'll be encouraged, too.

My credentials for your attention? My authority? I'm about to be initiated into that august, awesome role of grandma. And thus I'm ready, finally, to confidently pass on some of my hard-learned secrets of motherhood.

I'm not a knitter or even a quilter. So early on in my daughter Anne's pregnancy, I began fretting. Without these skills maybe I didn't have the "stuff" to become a bona-fide, picture-carrying granny. Maybe things have changed so much since my diapering days that my old techniques for burping and patting would fuel, not soothe, gassy tummies. This stack of "maybe's" ultimately catapulted me into a familiar heap at the throne of grace where, in my Moses-falsetto voice, I squeaked out all my inadequacies.

The Lord, of course, recognized my voice, yet he didn't buy my complaining. Instead, he countered with his grace—again. Tough, no-nonsense grace, the measure of which spurred me back on track with a nudge and a commission. This time it was simple: "Pass on what you've learned."

So bear with me. I'm feeling like the Titus

woman, that it is now time to hand down to my daughter—and you as well—the two best insights I acquired in the crucible of motherhood.

Like my friends, I read all sorts of child-rearing books—beginning with the now not-so-popular *Dr. Spock*—in the early sixties. I took classes at church and preschools, gleaned from my friends, treasured my husband's counsel, and prayed. Yet nothing prepared me for the trauma of toe-to-toe skirmishes with a teenager.

We've had four red-blooded kids go through this stage of life—and each one at some point brought me banging on heaven's door for help. But one day stands out above all the rest. The Red Sea parted that day, and while the wilderness ahead still held daily challenges, my motherhood badge was stamped "Delivered" from then on.

The day dawned sunny and clear. Perfect Seattle weather. Perfect day for Paul, our easy-going fourteen-year-old, to mow the back lawn, a simple morning project. However, as it dragged on, I was aware he stopped the mower more than usual and kept popping in to take calls on the upstairs phone. I thought nothing of it, except to note the grass clippings piling up on the stairs.

"Hey, Mom," he whistled on his way back from the fifth or sixth phone call. "Here's a permission slip for you to sign. I need your signature by Monday."

"Sure. What's it for?" I asked routinely, reaching to sign it without my glasses.

"Oh, nothing important. One of the school's

little forms. Just put your John Henry on the line. You can do it without your glasses."

Instinctively, I grabbed my glasses and started to read the document in Paul's hand.

"No big deal, Mom. I just need your okay for my locker partner choice for next year. Here's a pen. Sign away."

Face eager, he fairly panted, but his eyes evaded mine. I looked at him, at the grass clippings on the stairs, and signaled for time-out to finish reading the little yellow slip.

"Paul, you put down Linda's name for your locker partner. Why don't you go with Tom or Brad? Are you sure you want a girl for a locker partner? You may not feel the same way by next spring."

Sound motherly counsel, but Paul didn't like it. He bounded upstairs to the phone; I could hear his anguish from downstairs. Still, the more I thought about it, the "righter" I became. Suddenly we were locked in controversy.

"Mom, you've really upset Linda! She's throwing up. She thinks you hate her. Do you want to ruin our year?"

"I like you both," I protested, "but over the long haul, I don't think this is a wise decision."

That did it. We were in combat. Charges and counter charges. We weren't tangling over a big moral question; I couldn't comprehend Paul's reaction, but we were in deep. This was war—artillery and cannons. And I was the target. "Worst mother in the school. Old-fashioned. Stubborn. Heartless."

Inside I was crumbling. Caving in. Ready to weaken and sign the silly card. "God," I moaned, "you picked the wrong lady to be a mother. Four kids and I've just struck out. I'm not qualified for this job; I don't have what it takes for motherhood." I snorted and moaned as I held court with my complaints.

Then while absent-mindedly admiring the roses against the backdrop of the blue sky, two little words punctured my pity-party: *love* and *perspective*. How simple! So like the Lord to meet me in my emptiness and build me up, bringing hope. Of course he equips moms!

First, *love*. His for us. Redemptive and unconditional. And when received again and again, we become equipped to make tough decisions, to love despite rebuff, to hang in when the shots fly, to look discouragement in the face and choose to love back.

And second, *perspective*—that God-given long-haul view that comes with maturity and experience. We can love and train because we see the bigger picture of life; we know how much our kids need tough love, acceptance, and discipline to carry them through this broken world. We don't have to capitulate to the NOW.

Love and perspective. Two little words that also remind us of our Father's care for us. Hang on to them, moms. And hang on to him.

Coming
down the Mountain

eter said to Jesus, 'Lord, it is good for us to be here. If you wish, I will put up three shelters—one for you, one for Moses and one for Elijah'" (Matt. 17:4).

Peter, James, and John were on the mountain with Jesus. To be alone with their beloved Master was a rare privilege, indeed, but they experienced even more—the miraculous visual revelation of Jesus as the Son of God. No wonder Peter reacted as he did!

Who of us could fault him for suggesting that they remain in this surrounding atmosphere? Along with the others, he had had an encounter with the living God as he witnessed the transfiguration of Jesus right before his eyes. How could these disciples ever again contemplate the daily routine or the stresses of life "down the mountain"? How could they again be satisfied with walking the dusty roads of Israel, dealing with everyday needs of the sick and burdened people?

They had heard God speak—audibly. That's enough to make anyone fall face down in the dirt. And they did. Awestruck and terrified, the three disciples were laid low by the voice of Intimidating Love. Father God himself affirming his Son.

I love this story. A mountaintop spectacular

wedded to the mundane. First Jesus is glorified, and then he reaches out to touch the quaking men with two terse directions: "Get up," and "Don't be afraid." Not bad for men who would have to head down the mountain, who could not camp in the rarified spiritual atmosphere.

A descent down the mountain was inevitable. Life on planet earth was never designed to be lived out on a mountain peak. Jesus himself led the way down, knowing full well, we believe, that mountaintop experiences do not comprise the totality of discipleship. There was still the on-going commitment, the everyday "gutsy" choosing, the walking out of their real-life allegiance to Jesus' lordship. For the disciples this meant that they had no sooner "come down" from the heights than they were immediately involved with Jesus in the deliverance of a young boy.

Whether it is A.D. 33 or 1990, commitment must follow a mountaintop experience for the revelation of God to have its full life-changing impact. From the Mount of Transfiguration to the Rocky Mountains, this principle is still true.

I wasn't on the Mount of Transfiguration; but I have been high in the Rocky Mountains where I was treated to a descent that underscored commitment in a beautiful way.

Three of us were wending our way down from the eight thousand-foot level of the YMCA Camp in Estes Park, Colorado, returning to Denver after a marvelous weekend retreat. Great joy permeated the meetings. In the grandeur of that idyllic setting

God had met his people in a stirring way. Worship was rich in spirit and song. It was tempting to stay put, to linger on the mountaintop with friends who were also basking in the spiritually rejuvenating atmosphere. But eventually we had to head down.

To make "re-entry" easier and to savor the good time a little longer, we stopped at a quaint log cabin restaurant, the Fawn Brook Inn, where we could talk further about the weekend and enjoy a cup of tea and some Austrian pastry.

Our conversation would have continued non-stop if it hadn't been for the commotion at the next table.

"Don't miss this," our waitress urged. We all turned, eyes and ears taking in the scene at the adjoining table where a foursome, a younger couple and their elderly parents, were seated.

In a stage whisper the waitress gave us a running commentary.

"This couple has been coming here every year since their marriage to celebrate their wedding anniversary. This is their fiftieth anniversary, and their daughter and son-in-law are hosting the party."

A florist's bouquet and a simple white wedding cake decorated the table. The scene spoke of commitment in a way no sermon could have captured it. The wife of fifty years continually flashed an endearing smile to her beloved husband throughout the meal, occasionally reaching out to pat his hand. He, meanwhile, sat silently in his wheelchair, staring blankly into space and drooling saliva down his trembling chin.

According to the waitress, a disabling stroke severely handicapped the husband five years ago. "I wish you could have seen him before," she said. "He was one handsome man. They were a gorgeous pair."

But the tragedy of ill health was not the focus of this day's celebration. There was reminiscing over times past, joyful laughter about the stunts of the children growing up, gratitude expressed for the help given by the women of their parish in their recent need. This was no "pity party"; it was a true celebration of love and faithfulness.

Commitment! Fifty years ago a marriage covenant was established, a promise of love for better or worse, richer or poorer, in sickness and in health. Surely, this couple had had mountaintop experiences during their fifty years together, but underneath it all some significant choices had committed them to each other for a lifetime. This lovely wife was living out her choice to honor this commitment, even in what, to some, would have seemed to be one of life's difficult valleys.

Joy—contagious joy—surrounded this little gathering. Most of the patrons in The Fawn Brook Inn that afternoon left with moist eyes. We did.

It's one thing to enjoy the mountaintops. It's another to come down and daily embrace the ongoing commitment of God's call. We saw both sides of his call that day—joy unspeakable on the mountaintop and loving commitment in the valley.

Like the disciples we needed that full picture.

Being Somebody

*W*e've never regretted living across the street from an elementary school. Oh, sure, from time to time there have been a few incidents—like a baseball or two zinging through the upstairs bedroom window or tulips trampled to death when the fifth grade "scientists" retrieved their rocket project from our backyard. But over the twenty-four years, the benefits have far outweighed any negatives.

Not only did our four children have a glorious kite-flying, ball-tossing, safe field to play in, but we were treated to the laughter and squeals of hundreds of other kids doing what kids do best—playing.

Pretending, inventing, racing, singing, yelling—their "noises" rarely bothered us; rather they warmed our hearts. I've overheard tender and expressive apologies at the end of a soccer game. I've witnessed healthy kids cheer on handicapped classmates at special field events. I've seen teachers hug kids who always struck out in baseball. I've also heard heart-wrenching, plaintive cries. Like the one I heard from tow-headed Edgar.

The news hit the neighborhood three months earlier—Edgar's dad announced he was moving out—and in with another woman. Edgar and his mom left their old neighborhood and moved to a small apartment. From my vantage point as a "sidewalk superintendent" overlooking the school playfield, I saw Edgar's behavior change almost overnight.

His wonderful white-mopped head had always singled him out on the playfield. Now it wasn't his hair that caught my attention; it was his new solitary stance. He walked everywhere alone. Kids no longer hung on him, begging him to play. Coming and going to school and at recess, Edgar, the once-smiling, vivacious third-grader, was now always by himself.

This went on for weeks, until one day I heard him emit a blood-curdling screech. I was at my mailbox by the corner of the playfield when his voice pierced the air. I whirled around and saw Edgar locked in his teacher's massive arms, shaking with body-wrenching sobs. Somehow, in the safety of Mr. Matson's embrace, the floodgates finally burst. Head pressed against his teacher's jacket, he let out a piteous cry: "But I just wanna be somebody."

It made sense to me. Edgar felt like a nobody. In the last few weeks, one happy eight-year-old had plummeted to a new low. I'd observed the onset and his aggressively irritating behavior that invited others to back off. His emotional isolation spawned a vicious circle of rejection, and the pain was nearly killing him.

I was glad Mr. Matson was telling him that he cared. But you know what I really wished? I wished Jesus would tell Edgar that in person. That he would stride across that field, grab that tow-headed boy in his arms, look him in the eye and, in front of all his classmates, say, "Edgar, my son, YOU are SOMEBODY."

While we might not have had the emotional rug pulled out from us in quite the same way Edgar did, most of us relate to his heart's cry. We want to be SOMEBODY; we want to feel that somehow in this big planet, we count. We're not alone in this; the world is painfully full of people grappling with feelings of rejection and insignificance, searching for fulfillment to assuage their deep inner longings.

When we don't know "we're somebody," we're easily tempted, like some of our biblical ancestors, to cover our need for love by grasping for significance on our own terms.

Remember those Tower of Babel folks? They thought their brick and tar edifice could lift them above the mundane plains of Babylonia. "We'll make a name for ourselves," they insisted. Little did they dream that *Yahweh* wanted to stamp his name across their hearts, elevating them with true identity.

And Peter. How much he wanted to establish his reputation as Jesus' most loyal disciple. How much he wished his simple one-up-manship would earn him a special niche with the Master and cement his significance once and for all. Yet his strivings paled at the sound of the crowing rooster. God again had the last word.

"Don't blow your trumpets when you give

your offering," Jesus told the Pharisees. "Don't parade your pious prayers on the street corners," he insisted. He wanted to punctuate their self-righteous strivings with the truth that *they*, not their efforts, were of infinite value to the Father.

"I want to be SOMEBODY." Edgar's poignant cry is all humanity's cry. How can we count? How can we find significance? What will fill the vacuum in our heart? This desperate human search transcends all cultures and times. Unfortunately, ever since Adam and Eve, it usually takes us, not to Significant City, but to Empty Cul-de-Sac.

I've been in that dead end corner more than I care to admit. Stuck. Frustrated. Pained. Every time I've followed that old lie that I could earn my way to happiness or find meaning and purpose outside God's love, I've crashed against those restraining barriers and emerged hollow and empty.

Yet in God's economy, the pain becomes redemptive. Here Jesus rescues me with the truth: "Daughter, I don't love you because you're somebody; you're SOMEBODY because I love you."

CHAPTER THREE

A Touch of Grace

A bruised reed he will not break, and a smoldering wick he will not snuff out.

Isaiah 42:3

Tracking the Hound of Heaven

*S*he had a half-price coupon for a deli sandwich. I had a dollar and eighty-five cents. She had intended to hop out of the office for a quick solo lunch. I'd been stood up by a friend who'd forgotton our date. Recluse and orphan, we collided in the hall.

"How about a sandwich at 7-ll?"

"Why not. You wanna drive or walk?"

"I'll drive my van," she offered.

We were "on" for lunch. Hardly a formal invitation, but at that moment, for some reason, it sounded like high tea with the queen.

Yet 7-11 is hardly Buckingham Palace. More a hybrid between restaurant and store. Crammed with convenience foods, trinkets, magazines, and videos, an intimate lunch is unlikely. No place to sit, no gourmet menus, just steamy cases of barbequed chicken and humongous deli sandwiches.

"I can't eat a whole one," she said.

"Me neither. Let's split a turkey on whole wheat."

We plunked our money on the counter, and while we waited for our change, in walked Jesus.

Now hold on. We're not weirdos or even mystics. We didn't see Jesus—either in the flesh or in a

vision. In fact, we weren't expecting him, and as far
as we knew, he was back in our Christian office,
and we were out for lunch. However, when Love—
unmistakable Love—appears, you recognize it.

An unkempt, burly young man strode in
through the front door, brushed past us, and
planted himself in front of the counter. "Sylvia," he
bellowed. "Guess what?"

The girl behind the counter whirled around and
eyeballed the guy. The next second, her hand flew
out and grabbed his. "Hank, what's up?"

We froze midway in our exit toward the door.

And then eyes wide open, smile bursting across
his bewhiskered face, Hank breathlessly delivered:
"Sylvia, I've been sober for three days." Like a
preschooler giving his age he held up three stubby,
rough fingers and repeated: "Three days. Three
whole days."

Sylvia didn't even blink. She beamed unconditional acceptance straight into Hank's eyes like a
laser hitting its mark. One might have thought he'd
just told her he'd won the Nobel Peace Prize, and
she was congratulating him. But she only spoke a
couple of words: "Hank, that's great." Her gaze far
exceeded mere congratulations. Silent but emphatic
it said, "I see the real Hank, and I like him."

Despite the setting, we recognized it: Jesus'
love. And as if hit by lightning, we were struck
down.

I've thought often of Hank since then—knowing that even more than sobriety, he needs a Savior,
one with the *love* to accept him as he is and the

power to liberate him from all his sinful prisons. And I sensed that the Savior, the Hound of Heaven, Jesus himself, was hot on his trail—even in 7-11.

Jesus isn't picky when he wants to whet our appetite for his love. Lately I've noticed his tracks in unsuspected places—the movies, for instance. If you've seen the film "Driving Miss Daisy," you know what I'm saying.

In the final scene, the faithful black driver, Hoke, comes to the nursing home to visit his former employer, the arrogant, wealthy southern white lady, Miss Daisy. She shuffles to the dining room on her walker, frail, stringy-haired, no longer encased in her cocoon of upper-class respectability, no longer sharp-tongued nor aloof. Old age has won the battle over her social pretenses, humbling her with loneliness and confusion. But on this day she is lucid—and open.

Hoke's eyes meet hers and fill with tears. He asks if he can feed her. She nods her assent. The black chauffeur picks up a few morsels and gently puts them to white Miss Daisy's lips. Grateful beyond words, she responds in her halting, raspy voice, "You are the only real friend I have."

Talk about whetting your appetite for Jesus' love! That scene wiped me out. And even more. There in the theater, it propelled me emotionally to another "feeding" place—the Communion table, where Jesus faithfully meets me as my one true friend. Where he steps over my crummy pretenses, my self-appointed respectability and forgives it all, feeding me with his own blood-bought love.

There's something to be said for tracking Jesus' kind of love in unpredictable places. Especially if we let it smack our hearts and show us the cavern in our own souls. That God-shaped void that will not be satisfied with anything less than our knowing *"how wide and long and high and deep is the love of Christ—and to know this love that surpasses knowledge"* (Eph. 3:18,19).

I relate to Hank in the 7-11 and Miss Daisy in the movie. In those painful times when God exposes my neediness and strips another layer of pride, it always feels like failure and death. In reality, the Hound of Heaven is hot on my trail, nipping my heels with his relentless love.

Playing to Win

*B*zzzzzz! The deafening buzzer drowned out all the other sounds in the high school gym last Friday afternoon.

The gym was packed and the noise level, it seemed, was nearing the ultimate 130 decibels. The commotion was understandable, however, for this was the freshmen girls' championship volleyball game, and the kids, along with their parents and friends, were fired up for the big event.

I quickly found a seat on the visitors' bleachers, in direct line above my daughter's team and next to Betty, another team member's mom.

The referee blew the whistle, and the starter buzzer sounded. Our team, the Thunderbirds, and their opponents, the Chiefs, broke from their respective huddles where the coaches were dispensing last minute strategies. With a rousing cheer, each team yelled, "Let's go!" and dashed to line up on opposite sides of the volleyball net.

The first game went fast. The Chiefs poured on the power in a series of direct serves and spiked the ball so hard it was next to impossible to return. In no time at all, the Chiefs had nailed their first victory. Our "Birds" began to look a little droopy, knowing that they'd now have to take the next two games in a row to win the championship.

Both teams spent the first break huddled with their coaches. Betty and I saw our coach vigorously affirming her girls with encouraging pats on the shoulders. She must have sparked the hope that victory was still possible because they returned to the floor with renewed determination. Right off, their server fired six successive shots to the Chiefs' court with incredible speed and accuracy. From then on victory was in their hands.

The Thunderbirds were ecstatic, and so were their parents. But our comeback was short-lived. Only a few minutes into the deciding third game, the fire began to sputter. The Chiefs' first server earned them five quick points, and soon they were impossible to catch. Even when the "Birds" got the ball, they couldn't put it inside their opponents' court for a single point. The score was twelve to two. Our girls looked pretty grim.

Betty and I yelled our reassurance to them. "Come on, girls. You can do it." But realistically, we both thought the game was already decided.

The whistle blew for time-out. The "Birds" scrambled into a huddle. We tried to eavesdrop on the coach's instructions, but it was too noisy to hear much. Words like *ball hog* and *grandstand player* filtered out, and something about *working as a team*. Then we overheard the coach's urgent directive: *"You will have to cover for her weakness."*

We could hardly believe it: our coach was putting in Karen, an excellent server, but a girl who'd been out for two weeks with painful shin splints in her left leg. Shin splints aren't dangerous, but anyone who's ever had them knows they're extremely painful when you run.

Karen limped onto the court. Standing tall at the serving line, she winced with pain for a moment, then slammed nine successive fireball serves to the opposite court. The Chiefs were powerless to return a single one. Finally, after missing a serve, Karen had to assume the position right by the net. A vulnerable spot for someone with an injured leg.

We cringed as the next ball smashed right toward Karen. Before she could reach for it, however, three teammates were alongside her, tipping the ball back over the net. It happened again and again; Karen never had to move her painful leg. All she had to do was allow another girl to cover for her and hit the ball over the net. The "Birds" had come to life; they had become a team, helping each other at every play.

Our girls lost the game by one point that day, but everyone, including the other team, knew they had won a real victory.

Had Saint Paul been in that gym with us, I believe he, too, would have cheered for the "Birds." His words to the first century Christians were about the real life teamwork we'd just seen.

Those parts of the body that seem to be weaker are indispensable....But God has combined the members of the body and has given greater honor to the parts that lacked it, so that there should be no division in the body, but that its parts should have equal concern for each other. If one part suffers, every part suffers with it; if one part is honored, every part rejoices with it (1 Cor.12:22, 24-26).

"Ball hogging" and "grandstand playing" are not the "stuff" of a winning team, in sports or in the Body of Christ. As the Thunderbirds discovered in their glorious moment, we desperately need each other for sharing strengths and covering weaknesses. What is more, God needs us to be one. Paul's words are more than a suggestion for cooperation among divergent people; they are a mandate for the release of God's power and love in our world.

Traveling Light

*L*ord, I want to learn to travel light." It
was a perfectly natural request after
reading Eugene Peterson's *Traveling Light*, a challenging book on the freedom available in God's
grace. Little did I dream a firsthand opportunity
was just around the corner.

The experience began when I set out for a
women's retreat in Warwick, New York, with my
suitcase filled with clothes for two climates—chilly
New York and sunny Bermuda. I arrived at JFK
Airport on time, but my suitcase failed to show.

"No problem," the airline official assured me.
"We'll deliver your suitcase to the retreat center
later tonight when the next flight comes in from
Seattle."

I wasn't anxious. Between the efficiency of
today's computers to trace missing bags and the
determination of the airline to serve its customers, I
was certain my belongings would soon be on the
doorstep of the conference center.

Joan, who met my plane, was reassuring; she
too was confident my belongings would arrive. We
headed out through New York City's Friday night
rush hour traffic, minus my luggage, but light-
hearted and eager for the weekend retreat.

The next morning, however, my suitcase hadn't

arrived. Noon came and still no suitcase. I double-checked with the airline. The luggage hadn't been located yet, but the airline personnel assured me it would arrive by supper time.

Meanwhile, the retreat was in full swing. It was an inviting prelude for sharing on the grace of God, the theme of the retreat. Looking very well-traveled and wrinkled, I stood to speak.

By the second session we were focusing on the character of God, a Father who deals with us on the basis of his love and ultimate purpose rather than on our performance.

Jesus' death and resurrection has accomplished what the law and our own efforts failed to do: render us righteous before God. Still we, like the "foolish Galatians," are tempted to add something of our own to God's free gift. What a propensity we have for weighting ourselves down with excess baggage! We could all relate to that struggle.

Closing on that note, I phoned the airport again to check on the progress of locating my luggage.

Puzzled and apologetic, the airline agent admitted that the bag had not surfaced yet. I was still convinced it would be right along.

By morning I felt differently. This time when I phoned the agent was pessimistic. "Frankly, Ma'am, it looks like your bag could have been stolen. We've checked as far as Hong Kong, and we simply haven't been able to locate it."

Walking back to my room, I felt the impact of losing my belongings. I'd been in the same clothes for three days, and on top of that, I was headed for

Bermuda wearing a winter skirt. Here I was, a retreat speaker sharing on God's grace, and I was
having some very ungracious feelings—self-pity,
discouragement, annoyance, helplessness. Close to
tears, I reached for my notes and Bible and began
re-reading Paul's words on grace. Flipping to
Galatians I spotted a penciled notation in the mar-
gin—"Receiving grace is 'traveling light.'"

I recalled Eugene Peterson's book and my de-
sire to "travel light." *Well, Lord,* I thought, *this
wasn't what I had in mind.* It did, however, bring
more perspective to my dilemma.

I don't believe the Lord deliberately imposes
difficulties to make us miserable. We do live in a
world where airport conveyer belts malfunction,
and thieves steal others' property. We are not immune to the world's ills. Losing a suitcase is, after
all, a minor annoyance in the scope of life's events;
millions around the world never have the luxury of
any change of clothes. Nevertheless, at that moment, I needed God's grace; I had to say, "I'm bent
out of shape over this. God, help me."

A tap on my door startled me. Someone stood
holding two lovely white blouses. "Would you like
to borrow these for the rest of the retreat?"

"Would I?" God's grace was in the hands of
one of his daughters. The blouses were even my
size. I was humbled, grateful, and delighted.

Six months later the suitcase is still missing. An
inconvenience, yes, but it hasn't been all bad.

Frankly, to bypass the crowded baggage claim
areas on the rest of my trip was great. Without lug-

gage, going through customs in Bermuda was a breeze. I began to enjoy the freedom of not having to hassle with a big suitcase in and out of cars and airports, or not having to decide what to wear.

When Jesus commissioned the seventy-two to go out two by two, he said, *"Do not take a purse or bag or sandals"* (Luke 10:4). The pagans, it seems, were easily recognizable for their "loaded down" life-style. The hallmark of Jesus' followers was to be their simple trust in God's daily provision for them.

Traveling light, I was discovering again, involves the continual jettisoning of the excess baggage we carry—pride, self-sufficiency, our righteousness, anything standing in the way of receiving God's grace.

"It is for freedom that Christ has set us free. Stand firm, then, and do not let yourselves be burdened again by a yoke of slavery" (Gal. 5:1).

The Trip to Thanksgiving

*S*he wore her gray hair pulled back in a bun so tight it puckered her scalp. Except for a white linen scarf encasing her long neck, she dressed in dark colors. Usually black or grey. Never pink or yellow or scarlet or any of the colors seven-year-old girls want their Sunday school teachers to wear.

Variety was not a high priority with Mrs. Peterson. Her dress and her routine never varied. Each Sunday, she walked to the lectern, looked at her brood of second-grade girls, cleared her throat in a shrill grating rasp, and blew her nose into a purple handkerchief.

"Girls," she intoned, "we need to be thankful to the Lord. Let us begin with reciting Psalm 100." No surprise to us; we *always* began with Psalm 100. I did okay with the "come before him with joyful songs" part. I liked "we are his people, the sheep of his pasture." After all, I lived in farm country; I could relate to the value the Lord placed on little lambs. But "enter his gates with thanksgiving and his courts with praise" undid me.

For some unknown reason, when we hit that line in our unison ritual, Mrs. Peterson started pushing. Not physically but mentally. We could feel the "shove" in her voice and demeanor, as if she signaled giant herding prods to drop from the ceiling and corral us like rebellious animals. Her forehead furrowed. Her eyes narrowed, blinking out invisible fences to hedge us in. I knew instinctively that Mrs. Peterson had again set out to make us thankful. I, for one, decided I would not enter any gates laden with her baggage.

Sunday after Sunday, she persisted. Sunday after Sunday, I resisted. Each time we hit that one line, I went on automatic pilot and bailed out emotionally, locked toe-to-toe in a defiant standoff. No one was going to make *me* be thankful. Especially not Mrs. Peterson. My stubborn will inflated my sense of power; I had triumphed over my teacher's strategy.

I can't be too hard on Mrs. Peterson. For years, I adopted her same goal with my children, trying every ploy I knew to produce grateful kids. First the obvious: "Honey, say 'thank you' for the cookie." As they grew older and their good behavior became even more crucial to my identity, I inflicted them with the old "gun to the head" routine after birthdays and Christmases: "You *will* write that thank you note to Auntie Sarah. Or else."

Those stilted little notes may have impressed the relatives and even set a good precedent for the kids; but as couriers of genuine gratitude, they bombed.

Things *do* change, however. Despite Mrs. Peterson, despite my own stubborness, despite my misguided attempts to pound thankfulness into my kids, despite the evening news and scary headlines, somehow, amazingly, a gradual revolution in my perspective has occurred. I'd hope Mrs. Peterson would recognize it as the real item—thankfulness from the inside out.

My route to Thankfulness has been filled with more than its share of detours through Whiney Valley and Complaint City. Frequent breakdowns still occur on this highway and always will, yet Someone has been at work and my whole perspective is different. A difference worth shouting about.

Subtle signs of gratitude show up everywhere. In big things and little things, without any organ prelude or theological prompting, I'm feeling just plain thankful. Sometimes I get clobbered when I least expect it.

I'm sure you relate. A sunset explodes across the western horizon after days of monsoon-style rainstorms, and the whole scene knocks your aesthetic socks off. "Father," you breathe, "you have outdone yourself. What a Creator!" Overwhelming gratitude.

Your granddaughter runs down the hall, open-armed and squealing, to you, her grammy. At that moment, the house could burn down and the garden sink into the earth. All you feel is inexpressible thankfulness for another generation of fresh, exuberant life personalized in your arms. "God, you're so good!" It sounds like Pollyanna, but it's real— coming from your heart via your toes.

A valued friend and mentor dies and in the midst of your grieving, you are touched with undeniable appreciation for your relationship. The words come unprompted: "Thanks for Alice, Lord."

You find your car keys, a shoelace, or telephone change at zero deadline. A couple in an underdeveloped country shares their precious coffee and pieces of fruit in a barren apartment.

You cannot cheapen the moment with a casual thank you. Instead, you let your tears and silence speak. The list goes on.

I grew up in a tradition uncomfortable with "emotional outbursts" as we called them. A smile, a nod, a polite note—our tokens of thankfulness. I never dreamed I'd see the day when I'd say "Thank you, Jesus" spontaneously, whether in church at news of answered prayer or at the gas station when the attendant says, "One more mile and this tire would have blown." But that day has come.

So what brought about the transformation? The apostle Paul would say that, "God has done what the law (or Mrs. Peterson) could not do." His cross has exposed me—and continues to expose me—as an utter failure, yet totally accepted and loved by him. The progressive penetration of that truth makes every day Thanksgiving.

"Thank you, Jesus."

CHAPTER FOUR

A Touch of Presence

*The Lord replied, "My presence will go
with you, and I will give you rest."*
Exodus 33:14

Trauma in the Tube

We had only two days left to sightsee in London. And since no one wanted to talk about "countdown," we spent this particular morning eating in silence.

I reached for the last piece of toast from the silver toast rack, that inimitable trademark of a British breakfast. Without a word, husband Dick handed me the orange marmalade, sipped the last of his tea, folded his napkin, and cleared his throat. Daughter Gail leaned forward in her chair, squinted her eyes, and scrutinized her father. "Well, this is a hunch," she ventured, "but my guess is Dad has something on his mind."

After so many years, I no longer had to guess. I looked at my patient husband who'd held up for three weeks as the lone male in our group—a wife plus two daughters and a friend—and I knew: this man needed some space. The one who'd heaped luggage on carts in the train station, stood in line for play tickets, opened innumerable doors, waited outside shops, and calculated our monetary snags now had our attention for his announcement: "Ladies, I will be spending the day browsing some old bookstores—by myself."

We cheered him on. And added our own plans. The girls wanted another "go" at the British Museum, and I needed to pick up some gifts. An affable arrangement. We would spend a day apart and join for dinner together. Only one minor concern: Could Mom handle the tube by herself?

A ridiculous question! I was adamant in my defense. "Look, with my carpooling record and my nose for finding missing homework under sofas, I'm not about to be outwitted by London's Underground. If two million Londoners can maneuver through the innards of this city on little trains, so can one American mom. Of course I can do it. Trust me!"

Ever the caretaker, Dick cautioned me. "But, Honey, you really don't like navigating crowds, and you've been known to confuse right and left when following directions. Are you sure you'll be okay by yourself?"

"Enough. Off my case, Family. I'll do fine. I will be at the Russell Square Station at 5:30. And," I emphasized, "I may even be early."

And that was how we all left St. Margaret's Bed and Breakfast together, boarded the tube, and "split" for the day.

Shops and department stores along Oxford Street were jammed with people—tourists, like myself, and what for London was probably the usual crowds. Both intrigued and overwhelmed, I did my shopping nevertheless.

By 4:45 I had found Knightsbridge Tube Station. Packages in hand, I smugly eased through the turnstile, confident in my homing-pigeon instinct. Just as I swung my head to locate the descending escalator, the onslaught struck. From the left, from the right, seemingly from the sky itself, the hordes poured in with their shopping bags, their brief-cases, their umbrellas.

I was caught in the cross fire of the mass people-jam, bumped on the shoulder, elbowed in the back, knocked sideways by a guitar case, shoved by the bodies attempting to funnel down two narrow escalators. Somehow I got one foot on the moving stairs and hoisted the rest of me on, grateful for gravity and a five-inch space to grip the handrail.

I hung on for my life. This was no ordinary de-partment-store-variety escalator; this steep two-story job was overloaded with skilled riders who aggressively pressed in, over, and around. And noisy. It was as if someone had captured all the sounds of London, amplified them, and piped them into the tube station for the commute home.

Midway down I was jolted again from behind. I grabbed my parcels and felt my precious glasses sliding down my nose and myself getting dizzy. Like a tidal wave it hit me: Panic! Can I make it through here? Will I get squeezed off only to be crushed underfoot by the feet of hundreds of com-muters? Am I supposed to take the Circle Line or the Picadilly Line? My head spun and my heart raced.

"Jesus!" How automatic, yet incongruous, to say his name aloud on the escalator. But in my panic I said it again, "Jesus, help me, Jesus."

Then it came. Just before I reached the platform,

the unmistakable notes of a flute—beautiful, crystal-clear notes penetrated the turbulence. A busker, a London tube musician, played Bach's "Jesu, Joy of Man's Desiring." The music filled that cavernous station, swallowing my panic with it.

Jesus was in the tube station! The same Jesus who calmed the terrified disciples on the Sea of Galilee was in the London Underground calming one American mom.

"Where car I go from your Spirit? Where can I flee from your presence? If I go to the heavens, you are there; if I make my bed in the depths, you are there" (Ps. 139:8).

Where is the Lord we serve? Not far, friends, not far.

Caught off Guard

I found a new green spiral notebook on the kitchen counter yesterday. I knew who'd left it there. After thirty years of living with a list-keeper, chart-maker, full-fledged notebook addict, I wasn't surprised at Dick's purchase. Besides, I'd just picked one up myself.

"Man, are you guys predictable," observed daughter Jane with a resigned head shake. "I think you'd put the new year on hold if you hadn't gone out and bought your new notebooks."

She's right. Our record-keeping, list-making regime is too ingrained to scrap now. We're not going to miss a beat or be caught off guard by not getting our lives organized, at least on paper.

Notebooks came to our rescue a few years back. We literally woke up one day to the realization that we were slowly sinking in a bog of chaos. Between Dick's demanding job, the press of four kids' school and sports' schedules, gardening and house projects, and commitments to church and family, we were over-programmed, under-disciplined, and careening toward domestic gridlock.

One night Dick, who'd always kept lists on such things as the population trends of Afghanistan, the archeological digs in Jerusalem, or the heroes of the Boer War, suggested we attack our problem with pencil and paper. We couldn't continue to let disorder rule our days. In the privacy of the den, we made our pact: we would not be victims. No more would life catch us off guard.

"We'll rise from this muddle and regain control," I delcared, invigorated by our decision.

Then with a clandestine move, Dick bent over his briefcase and pulled out a plain brown wrapper. "Open it." He grinned. *He's been reading too many spy novels*, I thought as I carefully unwrapped the package, the first of our green spiral notebooks.

Nothing was off limits for that little book. We listed everything that filled our lives—our schedules for the coming week, family concerns, plans and dreams for the future as well as long and short-term goals, whether personal, spiritual, or physical.

Those lists hounded us. They reached out and confronted us with our own admitted priorities. And more. On paper it soon became glaringly obvious that we needed God's help. Before we knew it, we were praying first and listing later.

Finally, a semblance of order surfaced in our home. The extraordinary thing, however, was that while we finally seemed to be gaining a healthy measure of control over our lives, by the year's end, our notebook told yet another story: life was no longer catching us off guard, but the God of the universe was.

We had proof in our notebooks. We'd documented his quiet forays into our lives every week, not really apprehending the full impact. We'd simply chronicled his tracks as they brushed against our ordinary comings and goings. Hardly headline news or the stuff of miracles. Or so we thought at the time. At year's end when we read it straight through, the picture was mind-boggling but clear; we have a God who comes close.

Take a look at a few entries from last year's list: the offer of a weekend on the Oregon coast in a beautiful beach house when Dick and I were both exhausted; unexplainable rejuvenation from watching lingering summer sunsets and hiking beach trails; deep satisfaction from close, intimate sharing with family and friends; courage to confess hurt feelings and the subsequent joy of a restored relationship; the surgery nurse's reassuring words and her grip on my trembling hand; sermons that singled me out with hope or conviction; words of affirmation at the end of a dry spell.

I could go on. Someone else might call them serendipities, but I can't. They bore the unmistakable stamp of our Father's love—undeserved, unexpected, and precision-timed. I have to believe the Lord was, as usual, catching us off guard with evidence of his caring love.

We may have tried to organize and control our lives, but we couldn't corral God! He majors in catching this world off guard.

He sent his son to us via an uneducated, unknown girl who gave birth in a dirty cave. Then he announced this great news to motley shepherds, the society's lowest, most humble group. He called twelve untrained, unsophisticated, common laborers to be the first to pass on Jesus' teaching. And in a culture averse to women and especially to prostitutes, he illustrated his most profound teaching on love and service in his encounters with them. He turned the tables on the religious elite, punching holes in their self-righteousness to give us a true picture of mercy. Even death could not silence his love.

Our little green notebooks have ushered in some healthy order and control in our home. I heartily recommend them. But I look forward to another year when the Lord will continue to catch us off guard with his unpredictable, undeserved, and unrelenting faithfulness.

God at the Supermarket

*D*oes your carpet need shampooing? Have you considered storm windows? How long since you've had your chimney cleaned? Thought about aluminum siding for your home?

Sound familiar? Probably does if you live in a city large enough for telephone solicitation. And, if it's like our house, more often than not, the calls hit at prime time—dinner hour. I average at least four or five such calls a week.

Typically, I'm stir-frying veggies or grating cheese for pizza when the phone rings. The interruptions, by now, have triggered a conditioned response. I wipe my hands across the sides of my apron, head for the phone, and answer less-than-enthusiastically, "Hello."

Undaunted by my lack of cordiality, the salesperson plunges ahead with the latest pitch: "This is our finest offer. Prices will never be this low again." On and on it goes.

Like a robot, I come in on cue for this routine, "I'm sorry. We're not interested. Thank you."

Back at the stove, I resume dinner preparations while speculating about my caller. What's this person like on the other end of the line? How does she cope with the continual rejection she gets?

Last Tuesday at 6:15 P.M., I received three calls

back-to-back. Carpet cleaning. Storm windows. Pest control. (I must admit that last one was tempting.) I'd barely returned to stir the simmering soup when the phone rang again. Wooden spoon in hand, I retraced my steps, grabbed the receiver, and growled, "Hello."

"Carol, I hate to bother you at dinner time, but I've gotta tell you what happened to me today. I'll only take a few minutes."

I recognized the voice of my friend Bobbi. She sounded upbeat, almost joyful.

"Our soup can wait, Bobbi. Tell me, what's up?"

"You may think this far-out, but believe me it's true. Today while I was walking behind the university stadium on the path near the lake, so help me, Carol, God spoke to me."

What a change from hearing the pitch about clogged chimneys and aluminum siding that never needs paint! This was a call worth answering; it sounded like a breakthrough in Bobbi's long stint of illness and depression. I encouraged her to go on. "What did God say?"

"Well, it wasn't an audible voice or anything dramatic. I was walking by where the ducks congregate at the edge of the lake. I wasn't praying or even thinking spiritual thoughts. Out of the blue, the quiet presence of the Lord surrounded me. My ears didn't hear it, but my heart was flooded with an indescribable wave of love accompanied by the simple message, 'Bobbi, I love you.' Has this ever happened to you?"

I hesitated. More than once I'd been told how offensive Christians were with their insistence that God had just spoken to them. I knew people, in fact, who are so turned off by the words "God told me," they reject out of hand all the Holy Spirit's work in personally communicating the reality of Jesus' love.

Still, despite what might happen as a lack of wisdom on one hand or defensiveness on the other, the truth is we do have a God who works night and day getting his message out. He loves us! He is, in fact, relentless, stubborn, and dogmatic in his persistance.

Bobbi pressed me for an answer. I briefly told her of the afternoon in the supermarket several years ago when the Lord broke through a long spiritually dry and emotionally discouraging period to impress me with three little words, "I love you."

Like Bobbi, I wasn't doing anything unusual, just standing in front of the canned fish debating whether to buy tuna or splurge on crab. Also like Bobbi, I heard no audible voice, yet the inner impression was so strong I whirled around to see who had spoken. While I rarely mention it, I have never forgotten it. What is more, I believe the truth of it to this day—I "heard" the Lord.

Neither of these two incidents—Bobbi's nor mine—should be used to suggest the norm for our believing God loves us. In fact, we'd best stand guard against the devastating practice of demanding a spiritual experience to justify our faith. We are only too well aware of our propensity for emotional ups and downs. Experience can be ambiguous; we are called to be people of faith. Believers of the Word.

However, another side to this coin exists. God's message is greater than the condemning ones we often give our own hearts. He is committed to override the fears, the lies, the unbelief that assail us. When he determines to speak to his people, he does it—through a burning bush, through his prophets, through his creation, through his Son, through Scripture, and, yes, through a still small voice.

It's quite possible, I believe, in a world where impersonal dinner-time phone calls intrude into our homes and where we mentally replay old negative tapes about our self-worth, that the Lord of the universe commissions the Holy Spirit to give us his message—"I love you."

It can happen down by the lake or even at the supermarket.

CHAPTER FIVE

A Touch of Faith

*Let us hold unswervingly to the hope we
profess, for he who promised is faithful.*
Hebrews 10:23

Letting Go

I knew it was inevitable—if I were to keep my sanity. But I was the last to admit it: Wendy, our six-year-old springer spaniel, needed a new home.

We've had an "empty nest" now for two years. Except for weekends and summer vacations, our kids haven't been around to roughhouse with our dog. No lapping the school yard with her or placating her with nightly tennis ball throws. Although Dick and I walked Wendy faithfully every night, it didn't satisfy our hyperactive "love sponge."

Wendy was lonesome. Hardly a reason to "transfer" a faithful family pet. Except...except lonesome degenerated into boredom, and boredom opened a canine Pandora's box for all manner of doggie misbehavior. Such as tipping over neighbors' garbage cans, stealing lunches and baseball mitts from the school yard, taking naps in a neighbor's new car, incessant barking at the moon, scarfing down unattended pies or roasts, or inhaling dill pickles and olives from the relish dish on the table.

Impossible, you say? If you doubt me, ask my skeptical friend Diane who no longer scoffs. One night she popped into our kitchen just in time to see Wendy spring to the kitchen counter, extract one chocolate chip cookie from the cookie jar, and replace the lid. With Wendy, seeing was believing.

Amused? You're not alone. Our friends, *most* of our neighbors, the kids at school—everyone else thinks Wendy is a one-of-a-kind wonder dog. The funniest pooch they've ever seen. Incredibly creative. And of course, always lovable. I felt the same way. Except when I had to scour the neighborhood for her in the pouring rain. Except when I had to retrieve her from Duffy's Tavern where she entertained the customers by leaping for french fries. Except when I had to pry her loose from the junior high lunchroom on hamburger day, or identify her at the animal shelter forty miles away—on the snowiest day of the year.

Although I hated to acknowledge it, that twenty-four-hour-a-day dog was running in the fast lane and dragging me with her. Yet if anyone hinted that my life might be a lot easier without her, I either changed the subject or dismissed them as dog-haters. Privately, however, I sighed— deeply. After all, I'd grown up with dogs; they'd been my childhood confidantes. I wasn't about to let go of something that gave me so much satisfaction. I couldn't face the thought of living in a "dogless" house. So for longer than I care to admit, I denied the problem.

Freckle-faced Wendy, however, never connected with denial. She was too busy living. Being herself—one hundred percent. It would have taken a canine sleuth to track her down as she crisscrossed arterials, jumped over fences, even leaped through open windows.

But no doggie detective trailed her. Just me, one phone-weary dog owner, tired of hearing the same old message: "Lady, *please* come get your dog." The last angry call came at six in the morning. That was it. Enough. I'd had it. The joy of looking into Wendy's big brown eyes for unconditional doggie love was not worth this kind of hassle.

Without a doubt, our city dog needed a country home. And I needed to let her go.

Does our creator God of the universe have time to find new homes for dogs? I asked myself on the way to work. *Can he help one ambivalent dog owner part with her pet? Does he care?* I sniffled out my prayer request at Monday morning prayer. From the other end of the long table where our department gathers, quiet, confident Laurie prayed, "God, help Carol find a good home for Wendy."

"Amen." I could agree through my tears, but the pain began rolling in through my mid-section. Letting go wouldn't be easy; after all I'd been through, I still couldn't imagine life without a dog.

But, wonder of wonders, my dairy farm cousin wanted one. Somehow we connected. He needed a mature, kid-loving, non-cow-chasing dog. And Wendy needed what he had to offer—space, freedom, and four kids.

I dreaded transfer day. We loaded Wendy into our station wagon and headed up the interstate in silence, she with her unsuspecting nose on my shoulder, and I trying to block out words like "meanie" and "traitor."

Does our creator God care about dogs and their owners? Ask me. I'm a believer. Wendy and the farm clicked. The kids took her to the county fair where she won a blue ribbon for Best Family Pet. When I saw her swim in the pond and run across the fields with her ears flying in the wind, I saw beautiful freedom. "Go for it, Wendy," I shouted. And then we were both free.

When Jesus said, "The way is narrow," he was talking about entering into a relationship with the Father. But I believe he was also describing the dimensions of that new life. We cannot have it both ways. We can't be bound and free at the same time. If we opt for his love and his freedom, we'll have to keep letting go—all of our lives. Of everything we've attached to ourselves that stifles the expression of the person we were created to be.

And in his stubborn love, he'll keep moving heaven and earth—and dogs if need be—to help us.

Finding Our Way

*W*e wore hooded rain ponchos and carried umbrellas. Like intrepid explorers, the four of us—my husband, myself, and another couple—literally splashed through the gates of Expo '86 in Vancouver, Canada, to enter the 173-acre celebration of humankind's achievements in transportation and communication.

Undaunted by the May downpour and the cold winds whipping the water, we hopped across puddles, skirted overflowing downspouts, and systematically weaved our way through crowds.

Although we'd come for a much-needed three-day getaway, we were also curious. Could four unscientifically-minded people get excited about endless technological displays? Would anything in the stainless steel, plastic, and complicated electronic stuff warm our hearts? Would anything here encourage us to cope with life in the fast lane of our unrelenting determination to go swifter and farther?

We got our answer. But not until we were midway through all the exhibits and our minds had had two days of ricocheting between what was, what is, and what will be in transportation and communication.

For me, the Italian pavilion started it. I rubbed

my hand across the fender of a silver sports car. Ten minutes later, I gingerly patted the wheels of a second-century Roman chariot. From then on my mind and imagination were in high gear.

When I saw the model of the Pinta in Spain's exhibit, I visualized Columbus' sailors struggling with winds and sails to cross the Atlantic. I had a similar reaction in Hungary's pavilion; I pictured the pomp and ceremony accompanying their king as he rode to court in his magnificent horse-drawn carriage.

As I looked at the sleek, hand-carved canoes in the Philippine exhibit, I could "hear" paddles dipping through the water. In the same way I "heard" the familiar roar of blast-off as we toured the U.S. pavilion and saw the mock-up of a space shuttle.

A few minutes later in a commercial exhibit, we took a simulated ride in a vintage 1930s airliner. We listened to revving engines now antiquated. But when we stepped on the people-mover in the Washington state pavilion and were effortlessly carried past their multimedia presentation, the impact of our experience struck me.

Humankind's ingenuity and persistence have achieved incredible results in the last five thousand years. We couldn't stop with the invention of the wheel; we weren't satisfied with a primitive two-wheeled cart, good only for a short jog into the village. We kept pressing against new frontiers, challenging old limitations. Across the water. Over the mountains. Beyond the plains. Into the air. Finally, to the moon and back in spacecraft moving faster than the speed of sound. And we've not turned back. Our high-tech achievements whet our appetites to press on, to accelerate our insatiable quest of going faster and farther.

Heavy thoughts for someone on a holiday! I welcomed my husband's suggestion to take a break—especially since it meant lunch at the Belgium waffle stand. Like robots winding down, the four of us dropped into chairs, propped our feet up, and talked about simple things—the stunning beds of lavender-and-pink tulips, the parade of people in identical white rain ponchos, and whether we could ever remember a May when it rained so much. Talking about ordinary things with ordinary people felt good after hours of exploring other worlds.

A loudspeaker interrupted our conversation. "We have a lost little boy named Mark. Would his parents please pick him up at the Lost-and-Found Station?"

Not unusual—more than ninety thousand people were on the Expo grounds that day. Still we caught the irony of the announcement. On a site featuring the history of mankind's best means to get places, to get lost is still possible. Especially for a kid.

Although we didn't realize it then, we were on the trail to answering the question we came with: Would anything here warm our hearts? The full answer hit us inside the General Motors pavilion.

We walked up a ramp past an array of new cars and vans, but to our surprise and delight the media presentation inside concentrated on people, not things. The Kwakiatl Indian narrator talked about the needs of human hearts, the longings of our spirits, of things that made life worthwhile. Then with laser-beam precision, he posed the crucial question, "In all this mass of stainless-steel technology, where are we going?"

A lost boy and a penetrating question. Together this put all the evolution of humankind's marvelous accomplishments into perspective. Unless we know where we're going, how we get there is irrelevant. And we need to know we're lost, even amid our best achievements.

"How can we know the way, Lord?" Thomas asked Jesus two thousand years ago. And Jesus' reply still confounds the wisdom of the wise and outstrips the highest technological answers.

"I am the way and the truth and the life." The way for all us "lost kids" is a person—Jesus. May we rest in that Good News. And live like people who believe it.

Passing the Torch

As the Summer Olympics begin this July, thousands of avid sports fans from around the world will gather in Seoul, Korea, while, at the same time, millions will surround their TV sets at home to watch the highly-trained, well-disciplined athletes compete for new records.

Even if one is not ordinarily a sports' enthusiast, to be captivated by this historical "spectacular" is easy. As favored young athletes strive for the coveted gold, silver, and bronze medals, a sense of drama builds.

A special time for me is the opening ceremony. Show me the backdrop of waving flags, broadcast the national anthems of the representative nations, and I'm hooked.

Then comes the supreme moment signaling the opening of the games. The chosen runner swiftly carries the blazing torch across the crowded stadium and up the stairs. He turns, raises the torch high, and ignites the Olympic flame, the fire that will burn during the entire two-week event.

Coming directly from the site of the original games once held on the plains of Olympia near Elis, Greece, more than twenty-five hundred years ago, the flame has been passed from runner to runner, then to carriers on ships and planes, to more runners. Finally it reaches its destination, the nation's host stadium. Here it brings the message of peace and friendship.

Passing the torch is an expressive symbol exceeding words. I'm sure the athletes watching the entering flame must be as stirred at the thought of participating in this long history of competitors as they are at the idea of excelling in their respective sport. And while they may be competing in just one or two events, they are, nonetheless, a part of a historic continuum originating in 776 B.C.

Passing the torch. Jesus had this concept in mind when he answered the disciples' questions shortly before his ascension.

They had asked, *"Lord, are you at this time going to restore the kingdom of Israel?"* (Acts 1:6).

His answer typically caught them off guard. *"It is not for you to know the times or dates the Father has set by his own authority. But you will receive power when the Holy Spirit comes on you; and you will be my witnesses in Jerusalem, in all Judea and Samaria and to the ends of the earth"* (Acts 1:7,8).

What an unexpected twist! The Lord was not going to act independently of them. The Holy Spirit would empower *them* to be God's agents in establishing his kingdom. *They* were his plan.

The rest of Acts literally explodes. The Holy Spirit is poured out at the Jewish festival of Pentecost, and the Lord used Peter's sermon to sweep in three thousand converts.

We know the rest. Peter headed out to witness to the Jewish people. Paul was raised up as an apostle to the Gentile world. From one isolated spot on the face of the earth the Gospel fires began to spread rapidly. Out from Jerusalem, across the Roman Empire, the torch was passed from person to person, from town to town.

As present day Christians, we, too, are part of a long line of people to whom the torch of faith has been given. From the birth of the Church at Pentecost to the present day, this flame of faith has been passed along from person to person, from generation to generation. Sometimes the flame has flickered weakly over dark periods in our history, but God has never left us without his witness on the earth.

When unfaithfulness, heresies, or corruption in the ranks of Christendom prevailed, God would raise up a leader through whom he could bring renewal and refreshing to his people. We can count these torch bearers throughout the centuries—Augustine, Luther, Calvin, Wesley, Whitefield, Carey, Billy Graham, to name a few. But as powerful an influence as these great "stars" of the faith are, they alone cannot account for all the torches passed down through the years.

Fathers and mothers whose exemplary life and genuine love equalled their words of faith, grandmothers who prayed faithfully for kids on drugs, secretaries whose attitudes revealed Christ's character to their bosses, executives whose Spirit-filled lives illustrated justice and mercy to their employees, teenagers who invited other kids to join the before-school Bible study—all have been a part in passing the torch.

"Don't leave Jerusalem," Jesus told his disciples. "Wait for the power of the Holy Spirit to come upon you." This rag-tag, frightened group was given the key to becoming his witnesses throughout the earth and restoring his kingdom—"Be filled with the Spirit of the Living God."

It is our key, too, for passing on the flaming torch of faith to a desperate world.

Hungry

I have never eaten a horse. Or even horse meat. But I can remember a couple times in my life when I was so hungry I claimed I wanted to.

Maybe you recall those teenage years when you hiked for five miles, stopped for lunch, and discovered you'd left your tuna sandwich and brownie on the kitchen counter. By the time you'd hiked back, hunger pangs were playing a John Phillip Sousa march in your empty stomach, and you were certain they would transpose into a funeral dirge— yours.

You didn't die of starvation, although you'd convinced those around you it was a close call. Miraculously you staggered into the house and with one weak hand opened the refrigerator door, grabbed the jar of peanut butter, scooped out a large hunk and squashed it between two limp slices of Wonder bread. Life flowed back into your frail body, and you retracted your threat of eating a horse.

The truth is I've struggled more in my life with turning down food than not having enough. While much of the world goes to bed hungry at night, I've been surfeited with food, not deprived.

Slim pickings occurred sometimes between

paychecks in the early years of our marriage with four kids to feed, but basically Dick and I have always had plenty of food in the house. Enough for ourselves and any guests. And as the primary cook, my greatest satisfaction came when people sat down hungry at our table.

I wanted pleasure that last month for our Soviet guests who'd come to Seattle for the Goodwill Games. No big overriding agenda, but my expectation was certainly there; I wanted these two guys to sit down hungry and get up nourished and satisfied.

It didn't quite work that way.

Igor, the twenty-five year old, arrived first. Slim, athletic looking, he spoke passable English. After some initial unpacking he emerged from his room. *Aha*, I thought, *he's hungry after the long flight. He's ready for dinner. And so are we.* I made the invitation.

A salmon dinner, however, didn't tempt Igor. "I'd prefer just a glass of water and a chance to smoke outside. I'm not hungry."

He wasn't hungry the next morning either. I put out exactly what the Rotary Club suggested for a typical Soviet breakfast: cheese, cold meats, smoked salmon, orange juice, dark rolls. Igor, pleasant and conversational, picked marginally at his food. He drank his coffee and after a polite "sit," excused himself to the deck for a smoke.

Puzzled, but determined to roll with the program, I suggested we start our sightseeing at the Seattle Center. He enjoyed the view from the Space

Needle; he specifically wanted his picture taken in differing poses against the backdrop of all the downtown buildings. Between shots I found myself preoccupied with thoughts of lunch. *Doesn't this guy ever get hungry? I've had breakfast and all I can think about is food.*

"Igor," I proposed, "how about lunch in the Center House? We could eat and rest our feet for a few minutes."

He shrugged. Like eating was one of the lesser options in his life. "Sure," he responded and then tacked on a more pressing issue, "Can I smoke there?"

Since he didn't care where we ate, I beelined to Pizza Hut and ordered the usual. Fifteen minutes later I was eating a slice of pepperoni pizza while Igor nibbled at the edges of another piece and puffed on a cigarette. We were struggling to communicate. "What do you think of Gorbachev? What's it been like with Glasnost?" But the conversation never took off.

"Can I join you?" Sensing our communication struggle, another American, a Russian interpreter who was also lunching on pizza, sat down with us and immediately engaged Igor and me in lively conversation. Back and forth in Russian and English. We were finally getting through to each other.

Turning to me, John made a quiet aside. "I'm here with the Christian Outreach for the games."

My response was spontaneous. "Praise God!"

That's all John needed. He leaned forward and

spoke to Igor in Russian. "I'm a Christian and I have a gift for you—a Russian Bible. I would like to give it to you, but I don't want to offend you."

Light flooded Igor's eyes. His face brightened into a broad smile. He spoke eagerly, reaching out to receive the gift. This guy had come alive—at last—and he couldn't stop talking. "What's he saying?" Something big had sparked.

John grinned. "I wish you could hear it in his native language. Igor says he would *love* a Bible. A new openness is in the Soviet Union, especially among the young people. They all want to know the truth about God. He keeps repeating one phrase: "I'm desperate for spiritual food. I'm so hungry. I'm so hungry. I'm so hungry.'"

The cry of a hungry human always reaches the heart of God. Igor's reached mine that day. Without a doubt, he was spiritually hungry. And without a doubt, Jesus has set out to feed him.

CHAPTER SIX

A Touch of Truth

The truth will set you free.
John 8:32

To Tell the Truth

he whole room was mesmerized by the little woman in the blue silk dress. For forty minutes, Nien Cheng, with a quiet, commanding presence, told about her treatment at the hands of the Chinese communists during the Cultural Revolution.

I sat amazed looking over the crowd of four hundred people, mostly young career women. Fashionable, sophisticated, well-educated, I was sure most of these women frequently attended business seminars in plush hotel banquet rooms like this one. But tonight they seemed stripped of all their adult trappings. Like small children, they leaned forward in their chairs, eager to catch every word spoken by a diminutive seventy-four-year-old Chinese woman.

The irony was rich. The Joseph story all over again. From her cold, dreary cubicle in the Shanghai prison where she was interrogated and tortured for six-and-a-half years because she unequivocally continued to speak the truth, Nien Cheng has been catapulted to an international platform where people now stand in line to hear her share the truth. She has believed, spoken, and lived truth. In that room, that evening, Truth seemed to have a power and presence of its own.

"How could you keep your sanity?" "What kept you from just giving up?" "Why didn't you hate your captors?" The question period was electric; the audience peppered her, determined to pinpoint the source of Nien Cheng's indomitable inner strength.

This wasn't a "Christian affair." Nien Cheng hadn't been asked to give a sermon. But truth, humbly and compassionately lived out, opens its own door for further exposure.

"I prayed. I repeated scripture I'd memorized. I was willing to die but determined to speak the truth." Her answers came quietly, matter-of-factly, and seemed to fall on thirsty, incredulous hearts.

For two hours after her talk Nien Cheng autographed copies of her book, *Life and Death in Shanghai.* I overheard her hostess remind her it was late, and she didn't have to sign more than twenty minutes to make the crowd happy. Her reply was gracious but definite: "I will sign until the room is empty." The line was long; but people were patient, caught in the evening's perspective of what qualified as time well spent.

The woman behind me struck up a conversation. "Can you imagine what would happen if we told the truth all the time? I can't get over how she did that—just kept refusing to confess to crimes she hadn't committed. I mean, really, it was great, but not too practical for the rest of us."

The wheels churned in her head. This whole truth business had hooked her. She wanted to believe it, yet her whole life experience told her it really wouldn't work. Not in the "real world."

"You know what?" she volunteered. "I told a lie this morning when my neighbor wanted to borrow my iron, and I didn't want to lend it to her. I told her it was broken; that's a lot easier than having your neighbor get mad at you. Wouldn't you have done the same?"

By now we'd inched up to within a couple of feet of the autograph table. Close enough for me to see the scars on Nien Cheng's wrists—deep bracelet-like scars—reminders of the painful infections that erupted when her hands were manacled behind her back for days at a time.

I looked at the jagged scars and turned to the woman who'd asked me the question. The moment of truth had come. It was my turn to speak it—briefly, naturally, as much as this hungry heart could take. In this atmosphere, it was like pouring water on dry ground to say something as simple as, "I've done the same thing—squeezed truth, well, lied to free myself from someone's anger. But you know, Jesus says the opposite is true: 'Truth sets us free.' I believe he's talking about himself as the Truth. He's the one who makes it possible—for Nien Cheng and for us."

"Really?" She was intrigued. "I wish we could talk longer."

I've thought often of this woman's question: "What would happen if we told the truth all the time?" In fact, I thought of it this week; I nearly lied when a friend wanted to circumvent the rules of our tennis club and use our membership for the summer—without paying the guest fee. I hated to disappoint her and her kids. They could have three months of tennis playing. "Everyone's doing it, Carol. No big deal."

Everything in me wanted to capitulate to that eager, friendly voice. A voice that was soon joined with another all-too-familiar one: "Carol, don't be a prude; it's only a small favor. You're not going to grow a Pinocchio nose overnight; the club doesn't have to know. You're not going to permanently scar your reputation."

Scar? Scars? The enemy had overplayed his hand. I recalled Nien Cheng's scars, forged in the furnace of truth against lies. I remembered Jesus' scars. I remembered the price Truth paid. In the moment of my weakness, Truth came to my rescue; I opted for freedom.

It's a good question: "What would happen if we told the truth all the time?"

Breaking the Esperanto Syndrome

*I*f the word *Esperanto* doesn't ring a bell with you, don't be surprised. It is not a household word. Ludovic Zamenhof, a young Polish doctor, first came up with the concept of Esperanto, a universal auxiliary language using words common to chief European languages, in the 1880s. But high hopes that Esperanto might achieve a communication breakthrough across the world flopped.

Sadly, for the world and for Zamenhof, the idea never really caught on.

Now, a century later, Esperanto is little-used and vaguely remembered. True, a few books published in this language exist, and several international conferences used Esperanto as the official language. But a major, cross-cultural language revolution never materialized.

Zamenhof had high expectations. He believed one simple language could be *the* universal language, a vehicle through which people around the world could express themselves on equal footing. Speaking the same language would eliminate costly and aggravating misunderstandings and at the same time foster trust, mutual understanding, and goodwill.

I haven't thought about Esperanto for years.

Recently, however, my memory was jogged by a chance conversation I had on a flight enroute to a weekend retreat. A businessman across the aisle volunteered he was heading east to address several seminar sessions of a prestigious group of business people.

"And how about you?" he asked, observing the notes I had spread out on the tray in front of me. "Are you going to a seminar, too?"

"Not exactly a seminar," I told him. "A Christian retreat—for women."

"Well, if it's a Christian retreat, for goodness sake speak English," he said, with a trace of annoyance in his voice. "I can't understand the jargon and 'in-house' terminology *you people* speak."

Obviously, a touchy subject. I sensed his adrenaline was pumping as he vented.

He continued. "Pardon my forthrightness, but, frankly, so many Christians speak an exclusive and rather archaic language. What on earth does, 'God told me' mean? Did he speak in an audible voice? Did he send an angel with a telegram? Your language is like a badge for the spiritually elite; no one else knows what you're saying. You're speaking a Christian Esperanto. Can't Christians break this syndrome?"

I couldn't just write off this young businessman's comments as defensiveness or an overreaction to some past negative experience, although both explanations were possible. I'd been challenged to answer some hard questions.

How do we handle the Gospel, the best "Good

News" in the world? The question occupied my thoughts during the rest of the flight. Then, as we prepared to land, my friend across the aisle leaned over.

"If I were you," he said, "I'd concentrate on telling your story like it is. Forget the gobbledy-gook. Talk simply, naturally, clearly. Like your hero Jesus talked. No religious slogans, no cliches, no stilted Elizabethan English. And, wait, one more word of advice: Be kind."

Talk like Jesus and be kind. I'd heard the heart of someone who'd felt left out of a "private club" because he was ignorant of the passwords and the inside spiritual terminology. Yet, at the same time, I'd sensed a fascination and even respect for the way Jesus communicated.

Look at Jesus closely. He preached and taught in the vernacular of the day, using illustrations and stories from everyday life. We have every reason to believe his conversations with friends were natural and appropriate—and yes, fun! No ecclesiastical language, no compromising the truth. His words were (and are) loving and truthful at the same time. They penetrated hearts, challenged religious traditions, and expressed the unconditional love of his Father. Not everyone received his message, but not because it wasn't clear; some of the hearts of his hearers were closed and couldn't—or wouldn't—recognize love when they heard it.

The pagans in the New Testament projected themselves in loud and empty ways, like noisy gongs and clanging cymbals. We twentieth century

Christians may "sound" the same way when we slip into our exclusive "Christianese."

The Gospel isn't transmitted that way. God's *agape* love is kind, not proud, rude, or self-seeking. Spiritual jargon that fails to speak to others' deepest needs can't transmit love. Instead it makes them feel like outsiders.

We can speak in the tongues of men and angels, but we cannot communicate the Good News unless God's love is burning in our own hearts, and we are speaking simply, naturally, clearly, foregoing "special" terminology. Only then can we break the Christian Esperanto syndrome.

Irresistable Forces and Immovable Objects

*S*tress—I'll never have to worry about that," I told my husband confidently several years back.

Never having had much more than a mild cold or light flu, I was unsympathetic toward "stressed out" individuals and naive about my own susceptibility. As far as I was concerned, I was not a candidate. Immune. Consequently I was a little puzzled why so many people talked about their stress symptoms.

However, I now know something new. And, you guessed it: I learned it from firsthand experience.

To swallow my pride and "eat my words" was one thing, but to experience eight months of a painful muscle spasm in my back was another. Razor sharp, unrelenting pain, the kind that eventually pierces not only your muscles, but attacks your thoughts and your energy. Life suddenly wasn't a lot of fun. And neither was I.

Others have experienced pain similar to or worse than mine. In fact, my personal adventure into "Stressville" wouldn't even merit retelling, except the result was more than just the victory of a good recovery. It is the testimony of the Father's ongoing commitment to us, to expose our

111

misbeliefs and to reaffirm the truth of his love, touching us at our everyday address, where we live.

The assault was gradual but progressive. An innocent twinge evolved into a sharp pain radiating across my right shoulder and into my chest. Innumerable doctor visits, medication, back massages, exercise, bed rest, and much prayer didn't halt the persistent pain.

Finally, my sensitive, caring doctor, perceiving my discouragement, quietly engaged me in conversation. He began by giving me an example of an elementary law of physics.

"A heavy brick lying on the ground will resist budging under equally heavy pressure," he said. "But if the pressure continues long enough, the ground under the brick will begin to give way. Under continual pressure, force builds up and, whether a brick or a muscle, something's gotta give."

"It could be," he hypothesized, "that you're trying to move something immovable or at the very least, highly resistant, and the something that's 'gotta give' is you."

"You mean like the old song we used to sing in the fifties?" I recalled the words:

When an irresistable force...meets an immovable object ...something's gotta give, something's gotta give.

Healing truth at eye level where I could grasp it. A diagnosis in the guise of an old Johnny Mercer song ("Something's Gotta Give") spelled out the facts I needed to face. I was the force pushing against a couple of "immovable objects." Not only was I proving the physics law of force versus object, I was becoming mentally and emotionally drained as well. My doctor labeled it "stress."

What had started out as genuine concern for two difficult home situations had subtly escalated into a single-handed effort to remedy things completely outside my control. My anxious striving and bottled-up feelings, according to my doctor, had put my body on "red alert," tensed, and in a constant state of emergency.

The diagnosis, unfortunately, didn't eliminate all the pain overnight; even healing truth carries a sharp sting. To face our own humanity, to be responsible for our own actions isn't easy. It hurts to admit our propensity for controlling, our failure to trust God, our frustrations, and our angry feelings.

For me, the stress attack was doubly painful. My back felt it and my head told me, "You did this to yourself." The truth was that I apparently didn't believe God could handle those situations, so I'd taken up the cause myself. Anyone who's rubbed shoulders with a "Messiah Complex" recognizes the signs. My own misbelief, prayerlessness, and stuffed feelings had plowed fertile ground for a stress attack. And my back caught it.

While we may be shocked by our human failures and lack of faith, Jesus, the Irresistable Force, isn't. Instead, he is at home with our humanity, drawn to us in our need, loving us enough to expose our strategies and shatter our illusions that we can budge immovable objects.

His grace-filled prescription still administers hope and healing to people who know they need help, those who are weary and burdened. To them, and count me in, he says, *"Come to me...and I will give you rest"* (Matt. 11:28).

CHAPTER SEVEN

A
Touch
of
Openness

*Nothing in all creation is
hidden from God's sight.*
Hebrews 4:13

The Bones in the Closet

*D*o you remember when spring-cleaning was more than just a phrase? When overnight your home became the scene of domestic madness with Mom shifted into janitorial over-drive, scrubbing and mopping through the house chanting, "Clean, clean, clean"?

In my grandparents' house where I grew up, these housecleaning campaigns hit every spring—and every fall. We belonged to that special "twice-a-year" fraternity; we were *real cleaners*— a definite step above the "once-a-year" people.

Daffodils signaled spring-cleaning. And in the fall, the vine maples. When the first leaf turned red, the white tornado struck our house again. Walls, windows, closets, cupboards, and floors quaked under the seige. Grandma scoured, sanitized, waxed, and polished for two arduous weeks, using her special cleaning rags, cleansers, brushes, plus some elusive formula she called "elbow grease," which, I learned later, did not come from the hard-ware store.

Boxes of stuff were carted off to the Salvation Army and the church mission barrel. And that great exodus always made me nervous. I'd go to bed and dream about gigantic conveyer belts haul-ing out the homey things I loved—favorite pillows, dolls, blankets. I worried whether my cat would survive the purge or if some special books of mine would be snapped up and whisked away to Final Land.

Our kids have no memories of twice-a-year cleaning campaigns, of beating carpets over clotheslines, or washing every window in the house on the same day. They learned a whole new culture: countdown vacuuming before company arrives, emergency boxes for quick countertop cleaning, Saturday chores before allowances. They adapted comfortably to a "lived-in" look.

Besides not being world-class cleaners, we were, unfortunately, savers, people who hated to throw things away, people who reproduced more savers. This fall, Dick and I are facing the results of thirty years of saving. With the last bird flying off to college, we're into a major cleaning project, determined to be ruthless in disposing of our accumulated stuff. We've made five trips to the dump, hired a man to haul away an old sofa the salvage people rejected, and, whenever possible, stuffed our kids' remaining possessions in their cars.

Apparently the project has not been thorough enough. A friend dropped by who actually wanted something I was trying to give away. I took her up to daughter Anne's old room, flung open the closet door, then ducked as a large bag cascaded off the top shelf and crashed loudly at our feet.

"What's in the sack?" she asked. I understood her curiosity but was reluctant to explain.

"Oh, just some bones, that's all," I assured her

and attempted to change the subject.

She wouldn't be put off. "What bones?"

I had no option but to explain that these bones came home from college, relics from Anne's anatomy class.

"You mean you're keeping human bones in your closet?" she pursued.

That did it. The next day, I determined to get rid of them. A simple resolution but not so simple to carry out.

The garbage can seemed like the natural repository, and I had them almost stuffed in when Dick quizzed me. "Are you sure you want those bones found in *our* garbage? What if some dogs tip over the can before the truck comes?" He had a point.

I'd bury them in the backyard—the perfect solution. Or so I thought until I noticed Wendy, our digger dog, circling the area with an archeological project in mind. Then Dick raised another issue: Seattle's unresolved Green River serial murders, with victims' bones still being found in the city. Did we want to chance interrogation about human bones buried on our property?

The fireplace appeared to be my only answer. But as I bent over the grate and started to burn the bones, I backed off. These were, after all, the remnants of a person, a real human being. A sense of dignity and reverence won out over expedience, and the bones went on their way to a nearby college.

Old spiritual skeletons, it seems, are not easy to dismiss either. Shoved away out of sight, stuffed in our "keep-looking-good" closets, the bones of unforgiven sin, unresolved hurts or disappointments also have ways of bobbing out at inopportune moments, of falling out to call the shots in our thinking and responses, impairing our ability to love as Jesus did.

I'm tempted to shove stuff into my personal closet, calling it anything but sin. Are you familiar with the pattern? You slam the door shut, nail it tight with some good Christian-sounding explanation. Then before you know it, all this ushers in a time of spirtual impotence and, if we're honest, hypocrisy.

Extraordinarily, Jesus holds us in his grip even in these times. He is knocking on the door again, ready to haul the old dead bones out of the closet, breathe new life into them, and throw in a new heart and a new spirit to boot. If we'll let him do it.

Jesus and the B & B

*L*ike so many turnarounds, this one wasn't dramatic. No screeching brakes. No skid-marks on the road. No harrowing U-turns. Just the handing over of two fresh brown eggs from one neighbor to another. A natural, ordinary event. So typical of the arenas God chooses when he wants to sideswipe our human frailties with his redemptive love.

As usual, he caught me off guard. I wasn't dressed for a profound spiritual experience. The radio wasn't playing Christian music. The scene was "early-breakfast—jeans-and-dirty-dishes." I'd just popped the last cereal bowl into the dish-washer when the doorbell rang.

Betty, my neighbor, stood at the front door with that "save-me-a-trip-to-the-store" look we both understood.

"No problem," I assured her. I knew how it felt to be in the middle of mixing a cake and discover you'd run out of eggs. "Stay right there, Betty, I'll bring you a couple from the fridge."

In a flash, I zipped down the front hall to the kitchen, grabbed two eggs, and delivered them into her waiting hands.

"You couldn't get better service at Safeway," I gushed. Then I closed the transaction (and the

---

door) with the familiar supermarket seal: "Have a good day."

The ways of the Holy Spirit were new to me then, but my initiation began that morning in my kitchen.

"Carol, why'd you leave Betty standing in the front hall? Why didn't you invite her into the kitchen?"

No audible voice, no spooky music, just a deep, clear inner knowing. Clear enough to prompt a response, at least in my thoughts.

"Betty's a busy lady. She doesn't want to make small talk in my kitchen; she wants to get on with her baking."

"Carol, what is the real reason you left her standing by the door?"

This still-small-voice business, I was discovering, was not only personal, it was persistent.

"Okay, Lord," I conceded. "I hear you. The truth is that Betty's a Scandinavian housekeeper, and I didn't want her to see my cluttered kitchen counters this morning."

Even as I expressed it, I shuddered at the sight of three encyclopedias pressing flowers, a stack of old magazines set aside to clip recipes from, and a jar of peanut butter left out from making the kids' sandwiches.

Betty's counters were always *clear*—and waxed.

"What are you afraid of?" The questioning pressed on.

Enough, I thought. I quietly terminated the conversation. Not for long, however. I couldn't bear the silence of the kitchen and the unsatisfied feeling

122

of stuffing an issue instead of resolving it. Besides I was starting to feel something else—a pain in my midsection.

"All right, I surrender, Lord. I'm afraid that if Betty sees my counter she won't like me."

"And so you defended yourself at the price of not receiving her. Self-protection isn't love, Carol."

Pow. I felt penetrating, pristine truth zing across my court, faster and more accurate than any tennis ball I'd ever encountered. I'd just been aced, but not by condemnation—by liberating love.

What does it mean to love people? To open ourselves and our homes to others? What's true hospitality? I've asked myself those questions often over the years since that egg exchange.

And slowly the picture is becoming clearer, especially after a recent trip Dick and I took through New England via all sorts of B & B's.

The hosts of bed and breakfast places uniformly amazed us. They literally "opened" themselves and their homes for our comfort and rest. One hostess in Boston had fresh flowers in our room, travel guides on our nightstand, hand lotion and extra shower caps in the bathroom, even a robe in case we'd forgotten ours. And like our hosts all along the way, she served us breakfast on "company" dishes—the family's china—and orange juice in their best crystal.

From Cape Cod to Maine, Dick and I couldn't get over the personalized care, how superior in thoughtfulness to most hotels. The lovely amenities, however, didn't ultimately captivate us. The people did—the openness of our hosts. They pulled up chairs in the dining room and joined us for coffee; they showed us pictures of their children or grandchildren, asked us about ours, let us see the kitchen and the rest of the house. In a word, they risked letting us "in."

Jesus must have sensed this atmosphere at Mary and Martha's place in Bethany. Apparently he felt comfortable there in spite of their imperfections. I wonder if Luke doesn't give us a clue when he writes: *"As Jesus and his disciples were on their way, he came to a village where a woman named Martha opened her home to him"* (Luke 10:38).

Openness. It is, I'm discovering, the key to true hospitality and real love. Sharing our home and a couple of eggs is good, but if we withhold ourselves in the process, it isn't enough.

Jesus never kept people standing empty-handed in the front hall to protect his image as the Son of God. Instead, he emptied himself of pride and aloofness and chose to be vulnerable, even to death. Real love, Jesus' kind of love, opens up. It lets people in.

Can we settle for anything less?

Out of Hiding

The September sunlight filtered through the trees on the Prinsengracht, a quiet street along the canal in Amsterdam, Netherlands. My husband and I stood on the street's edge with a group of other eager tourists, waiting to enter Number 263, The Anne Frank House.

Wedged tightly in a row typical of the older Amsterdam neighborhoods, this house stands out as a landmark, made world-famous through the writings of a thirteen-year-old girl. Millions have read Anne Frank's incredibly perceptive diary chronicling the twenty-five months in which the heroic Frank family and four other people hid here, in continual fear of being arrested and hauled off as part of Hitler's mass plan to exterminate the Jews.

For us waiting outside the house that September day, life was comfortable and pleasant under the warmth of the autumn sun. Jovial tourists struck up animated conversations, laughing and joking as they anticipated this stop.

From our place in line, Dick and I watched people leave the building. "Everyone looks pretty somber," he observed. I agreed. Their faces mirrored disbelief and horror. Then, we went in.

Immediately we were transported back to early 1942. That's when Mr. Frank started bringing in a few household effects, bit by bit to the rooms above the warehouse, as he prepared to take his family into hiding. Shortly they—Mr. and Mrs. Frank and their daughters—moved in, joined later by the Van Daans and their son, Peter. The accommodations were primitive, and life, restrictive. A heavy bookcase marked the entrance to the area. To even turn on the faucet or use the water closet until the employees of the office below left at 5:00 P.M. was dangerous. During daytime they'd had to draw the shades and walk on tiptoe across the rooms. A dark, silent existence.

The Franks and the Van Daans were bright, creative people, and Anne's diary records their valiant efforts to live normally in hiding. They were ingenious and determined to carry on by playing games, listening to music, talking together, and celebrating holidays and birthdays.

As Dick and I walked from room to room, we saw their cramped, dark quarters and were overwhelmed by the conditions in which they lived. Not only did they suffer daily deprivations, but overcrowding and bouts of intense fear as well. While this "home" was their only chance for survival, it was nevertheless a prison, and they were prisoners.

Neither Dick nor I could say a word as we left the tour. We walked away from the house speechless, gripped by the tragic reality that liberation had come too late for these people. Afterwards, our own freedom seemed loose and extravagant. Here we were, free to be gawky tourists and then free to walk away unencumbered.

Ever since we stepped out that door I've had a heightened appreciation for Jesus' ministry as a liberator who calls us out of hiding.

Self-preservation is a powerful instinct in human beings. My first reaction when I'm threatened in any way is to hide. Like the Franks, I want a refuge. Most of us have never had to hide in the upstairs of an old warehouse or in mountain caves such as the Israelites did when the fierce Midianite army ravaged their homes and stole their cattle (Judges 6). Yet we can relate to other kinds of hiding—hiding our true feelings from each other, hiding our fears and weaknesses because we're afraid we'll be rejected if others really know us.

Living in a fallen world and inheriting a sinful nature has left us—all of us—vulnerable to hurt, disappointment, and rejection. The fear of more trauma tempts us to run for cover. And, speaking for myself, that strategy always frustrates my true need—to be known and accepted just as I am—"warts and all."

Only when we encounter the extraordinary love of Jesus, the Great Liberator, do we dare to entertain the possibility of true freedom. What great joy to discover that the Gospel really is good news, that the Shepherd has been searching for us all along, and that he came to earth on a mission to release us from our hidden prisons. Incredibly, this stubborn Shepherd can find us even in our hiding places!

But old patterns and habits are entrenched, and

even after we know the Liberator we often fail to grasp the full dimensions of his freeing power. In our head maybe, but not in our heart. Our fears die slowly, and coming out of hiding, we discover, is risky business. I find it scary to rip off my mask and let you know who I really am. The greatest tragedy is that as a mask-wearer I cannot be an open channel of God's love to a hurting, desperate world. And I will not know true joy.

The world doesn't need any more phonies: it will continue to produce its own. What the world needs and what God wants are Christians who will come out of hiding, who will stand up and admit they're human, who will let go of pride, give up their self-righteousness, admit their needs, and risk their reputation—all in order to love. In short, God wants "real" people, ordinary sinners who've discoverd the safest hiding place in the world is in the arms of the waiting Father.

Count me in with those folks.

CHAPTER EIGHT

A
Touch
of
Courage

*Fear not, for I have redeemed you; I have
summoned you by name; you are mine.*

Isaiah 43:1

Coming up Roses

*T*hree years ago I promised myself a little rose garden in the backyard. Not that we were bereft of flowers or shrubs—we had plenty. But like most families with kids, we'd landscaped our backyard with the usual Northwest fare—rhododendrons, junipers, barberry—hardy plants to withstand the onslaught of stray soccer balls, the crunch of badminton players' feet, or the assault of a ball-chasing dog. Now in our near-empty-nest era, I could plant something more fragile, something with color and fragrance—something like roses.

At first, I wanted just a couple of bushes. However, each June when roses filled Seattle yards and flower markets, my little dream grew bigger. In fact, even in the dead of winter when no one mentioned gardening or planting, my dream refused to hibernate.

Instead it quietly bloomed inside me, propelling me to such covert activities as ripping out pictures of rose beds from garden magazines and fantasizing about hybrid tea roses.

Once I thought I could almost smell them when I looked out our sliding glass door across to the weed-infested, frozen spot where I knew destiny and my dream would one day intersect to produce a botanical wonderworld, alias my rose garden.

Red roses, yellow roses, prize-winning pink roses, the promise to myself escalated. The more I thought about roses, the more I wanted. The idea of an occasional fresh rose in my kitchen window no longer satisfied me; I now wanted roses to fill our garden space to capacity, and roses to fill not only our vases but our friends' and neighbors' as well.

I hinted to my family. "If you're running short on gift ideas, why not spring for a rose bush this year?" And bless 'em, they did. Roses rolled in— three from our kids on our wedding anniversary, two for my birthday, an extraordinary red one from husband Dick on Mothers' Day. The word was out; I was to become a bona fide, card-carrying rose grower.

One by one I hauled the burlap-wrapped bundles across the deck, shoveled deep holes, centered them gingerly, fertilized them thoroughly, saturated them with water, and stomped the loose soil around them. Full speed ahead: Roses! They had to grow if they were to outdistance my imagination, which was already in high gear.

I could hear the inevitable "oh's" and "ah's" that would greet my first harvest. I could see my sick friends' faces when I staggered to their bedsides, my arms overflowing with gorgeous, fragrant roses. They would, I was sure, lean weakly on their elbows and gasp, "These are from *your* garden?" and then recover immediately.

But alas, dreams and reality have a way of colliding midair in the upper stratosphere of our expectation. I had a big, beautiful dream, but I'd failed to count the cost. I'd promised myself a rose garden, yet I hadn't reckoned with any problems.

Like aphids, for instance. While we were on vacation, they came in hordes with their ravenous appetites. Unannounced and uninvited, they feasted voraciously on my fledgling rose bushes' leaves.

And dogs. Our own Wendy—the traitor—led the neighborhood canines in systematically digging for imaginary tennis balls planted in clusters under each rose. They exposed root systems, split off tender branches, and uprooted plants.

And mildew. And early frosts. And thorns that gashed my hands when I tried to prune without gloves.

To date I've lost four roses, including "Sterling Silver," a special twenty-fifth anniversary gift. Three others are limping along and will probably give us only a few buds this June. Bit by bit my dream has shattered, fallen limply to earth next to my pruning shears, my garden gloves, and my dirty tennis shoes. Yet in the shambles of all my smashed hopes, I've learned something about rose gardens and promises and the power of the cross.

One morning as I stood wincing over the remnants of my pitiful little rose bushes, I remembered a song from the early seventies—"I Never Promised You a Rose Garden." Jesus himself seemed to bump my elbow to remind me of his warning to his disciples before he sent them out: *"In this world you will have trouble"* (John 16:33). Yes,

Jesus, who promises us abundant life, never says it comes trouble-free. He isn't out to discourage us, but neither is he after blind commitments that expect only blessings.

I was getting a refresher course: growing roses isn't a trouble-free project, and neither is following Jesus. We are naive and foolish if we believe loving is easy, that trusting is simple, that forgiving those who've hurt us is a snap. No, the aphids, thorns, and killing frosts of our little garden-worlds come in many forms—misunderstandings, hurts, rejections, ridicule.

Jesus, the Rose of Sharon never promised us a rose garden. But he did say, *"Take heart! I have overcome the world"* (John 16:33), and with that promise, made in the shadow of the cross, we, too, can be overcomers—in him.

The Transformation of Ursula

From the start, it was a dangerous combination: a lunch hour with my daughter-in-law, a gourmet salad, and a walk past the bookstore. The inevitable setup for one of our animated conversations about a great mutual love—our cats.

I needed a medical update on Concord, Ginny and Paul's black cat who'd been rushed three hundred miles across the mountains for surgery at Washington State University's vet school. Ginny filled me in, her face glowing with hope now that Concord was surviving his car encounter, albeit with a limp and some metal pins in one hind leg.

"Only another cat-lover would understand why we go to such lengths to keep him," she explained. "Wouldn't you do the same for Felix and Ursula?"

I hedged. "Well, I'm not sure. We've had a lot of cats over the years, and I guess one gets a little more philosophical about their comings and goings, especially when children come along."

Even as I said it, I hoped I hadn't dampened her unflappable determination to vote—and act—in favor of nurturing and saving life. I loved her fighting spirit. As we talked, I could see her as a mom someday, dressed in a tiger suit and battling for her kids with that same winsome tenacity.

But we weren't through with cats yet on that

135

lunch hour. On the way back to the car, the book-store grabbed us by the throats—or so it seemed—and catapulted us inside. Magnetized by their front window display of cat books, we giggled our way through antiphonal title-reading: *Vanity Fur, The Black Cat Made Me Buy It, The Cat Who Ate Danish Modern, Cats Know Best, and Never Take Your Cat to the Salad Bar.*

As we exited, Ginny turned and posed a challenge: "Why don't you write something about Felix and Ursula?"

Somehow Wendy, our springer spaniel, always upstaged our cats when it came to writing stories. After all, two quiet felines were hardly a match for a rambunctious tree-climbing, counter-jumping, car-top-sitting dog. Wendy's whole life-style lent itself to making points about spiritual growth—forgiveness, patience, acceptance, etc.

However, Ginny planted a seed that afternoon. The offshoot is a real-life anecdote about Ursula, our beautiful longhaired calico.

Ursula came to us from "the other side of the tracks." Literally from a house being razed to expand one of our county dumps. My husband and daughter Jane came home from a garbage-dumping trip with her—a pitiful, whimpering lump of orange and black fur. I can still hear Jane flying into the house screeching, "Look, Mom, a lady gave us a free kitty."

She was free, of course, but also sick and filthy. Before the day was over, she'd upped her worth considerably with a trip to the vet for shots, pills, and a flea bath.

Ursula, we soon realized, had more problems than being sick and dirty—she was the original 'fraidy cat. When Wendy barked, she hid behind the sofa. She shook when the dishwasher ran, hyperventilated when we vacuumed, scooted under the table when the phone rang or we sneezed. She was, in fact, just plain afraid of life.

I wanted to pity Ursula; but to tell the truth, I was often annoyed and repelled by her neediness. Consequently, I grew to overlook her and directed my attention to Felix, our drop-in cat. Felix, the consummate feline charmer. She always knew where to sit, what to do, when to move, who to brush by. Never intrusive. Subtle, attentive, clever, sensitive to our moods: all the attributes that naturally attract one to animals—or people.

But five months ago, our whole cat picture changed. Ursula underwent a major transformation. Today she's a different cat. She nudges Felix at their dish; she invites herself on the family room sofa; she even stands her ground with Wendy over a choice morsel. She now conducts herself like a cat who knows who she is and what her life is all about. Like Pinocchio and the Velveteen Rabbit, she's become real. Seven years of being traumatized by life didn't sentence her to a lifetime of fear.

So what happened to 'fraidy cat? Her transformation started with our kitchen remodeling. When the bulldozer and the jackhammers arrived that first day, Ursula fled to the garage. For days the house shook; the windows rattled; the noise level accelerated past anything Ursula had ever feared. She disappeared for long stretches, surfacing only for late-night forays to her food dish.

Noises terrified Ursula. If she could have read the Bible, she would have understood Job 3:25: *"What I feared has come upon me; what I dreaded has happened to me."*

Then, one morning, she reappeared to do an amazing, inexplicable thing: she walked right out where the builders were hammering and sawing and sat down in the midst of the construction chaos. I couldn't believe my eyes. "Ursula!" I called in my protective, rescuing voice. But she merely blinked; she wasn't needy anymore. All day she stayed in one spot, like a feline foreman overseeing the sawdust turmoil. She didn't flinch a muscle. No longer a 'fraidy cat, she'd become a lioness, at least inside. And more than that, she was free.

I love Ursula for what she's shown us. She chose to face her fears and step through them. Jesus urges us to make that choice as well, to resist fear's paralyzing grip on our lives by acknowledging and repenting of our failure to trust him. The Amplified Bible catches his imperative voice: *"Do not let your heart be troubled, neither let it be afraid—stop allowing yourselves to be agitated and disturbed; and do not permit yourselves to be fearful and intimidated and cowardly and unsettled"* (John 14:27).

I don't know what motivated our calico cat to make the choice that transformed her, but I know that the Holy Spirit is at work, empowering us in our weakness to make that same choice—every day.

CHAPTER NINE

A Touch of Mercy

Mercy triumphs over judgment!
James 2:13

Mercy at Midnight

I wish you could hear our neighbor Chuck tell one of his stories. You'd see his hazel eyes shine, you'd feel the compassion resonating through his rich, deep voice. Lanky, long-limbed, lover-of-the-outdoors, Chuck isn't one to parade his faith. No testimonies where he emerges as Saint Charles. No miracles featuring himself as the hero. That's just not Chuck.

Yet after you've spent time with this struggling, transparent pilgrim, you come away refreshed. Like the Lord's hand has reached right through Chuck's heart to yours, injecting it with a gigantic shot of *agape* love.

Chuck's job with the university takes him around the world. His is a stressful schedule, filled with long night flights, jet lag, and culture shock. But it has its pluses: time to think, time to pray, time to badger God about how his life could "really count."

Making his life count. That's Chuck's theme song. Amazingly, we never tire of hearing him play that same tune. Like a maestro addicted to great music, he loves to express his heart's passionate symphony: How can his life be a ministry? How can he be a neighbor to those in need?

Recently, Chuck was barbecuing oysters for us

at their beach place on Puget Sound. He struck up the familiar music. "With all the overseas trips I've taken, with all the poverty and sickness I've seen, I'm convinced the Lord wants me to help the hurting. But I'm overwhelmed with the magnitude of it all. How can we know what he *really* wants us to do? What can we do that would make a difference for the kingdom?"

His wife grinned, shook her head, and rolled her eyes. "Honey, why don't you stop asking questions and tell the Greenwoods what happened here last Sunday night?"

So while the tide eased in across the sand, Chuck told us his adventure from the previous weekend:

"Paul, our neighbor, and I were sitting right out here on the beach poking the bonfire, waiting for it to die out. It was late, close to midnight, and Barb had already gone into the cabin for the night. The water was unusually still. Without a moon, it was pitch black. We started talking about how we could serve people in a way that could make a difference. Could God use us to help people in a significant way? How?

"We were tossing around a lot of ideas, trying to get a fix on what avenues of service would be open to us, given our ages and circumstances. Both of us were aware of noises out on the Sound, but that's not unusual for Sunday night. The channel is often filled with boaters heading in after a weekend, partying all the way back to Seattle. We never gave it a second thought.

"But during a gap in our conversation, I thought I heard someone yelling. We walked to the water's edge and listened again. I told Paul, 'Someone's calling for help. Can't you hear it? We'd better get the boat and check this out.'

"Paul didn't hear a thing. In fact, he warned me, 'Chuck, it's too dark out there. No way should we head out in your little ten-foot Livingston. We need more than a nine-horse motor—we need a spotlight and a bigger boat.'

"I was more sure by the moment: someone *was* calling for help. I couldn't risk waking up in the morning and finding a body washed ashore in front of our cabin because I hadn't made any effort to help. I had to try. I told Paul I was heading out, even if I had to go alone. But I didn't. Paul pulled the boat into the water while I grabbed a flashlight and a rope from the house.

"We moved out in the direction of the noises, zigzagging our way through the darkness. It was like looking for the proverbial needle in the hay-stack. We'd shut off the motor, listen to determine the direction of the cries for help, then start up again, going toward the voices. They'd yell, 'Help!' and we'd yell back, 'We're coming, we're coming!'

"Finally we connected: two men, one a big 260-pounder, the other a little guy, were clinging to their swamped kayak. The little guy, doubled over in a fetal position, had already passed out from hypothermia.

"I can't tell you how we rescued these guys. Another neighbor came alongside in his boat; but even so, the logistics were impossible. You just don't haul a 260-pound, six-foot, five-inch guy over the bow of a little dinghy—not unless maybe there are a few angels around boosting him in and steadying the boat."

Chuck finished telling us his story—how they called the medics, showered the men, rubbed them down, and put them in warm sleeping bags while waiting for the aid car. Two lives saved. Not on the dusty road from Jericho to Jerusalem, but on the waters of Puget Sound. Two men rescued. Not by those who passed by on "the other side." Not by those with all the answers on what constitutes ministry. But by those whose hearts beat with the Father's love. Those open and available. Those who have mercy.

I don't worry about Chuck's finding ways to serve the Lord. He's got the Good Samaritan story past his head and emblazoned on his heart. He's caught the point of the parable: we serve God—*right where we are*—when we act with the same mercy we've first received from him.

It's through lives like Chuck's that I clearly hear Jesus' words to me: "Go and do likewise."

Surprised by Mercy

*T*reacherous turn or harrowing hill—
sounds like a couple allegorical streets
out of *Pilgrim's Progress*. But they're not. They're
simply homegrown names for a hilly section of
road in our suburban Seattle neighborhood—a
stretch that has become notorious for its accident
record.

Rarely referred to by its proper name, Carlyle
Hall Road, this particular piece of road has had a
distressing number of accidents, including several
fatalities. The most recent one involved three teenagers coming home from the beach one afternoon.
The driver, forgetting to slow down at the top of
the hill, failed to negotiate the curve and the car
flipped over in midair, landing upside down in
someone's front yard. Two kids were killed.

Since then the police have responded to the
neighbors' plea to patrol the area and enforce the
twenty-five-mile speed limit.

I drive that stretch several times a week, and I
was thrilled that police were attempting to halt the
excessive speeding. Although the speed limit is
conspicuously posted in several spots, it's easy to
forget to slow down from the previous thirty-five-
mile-an-hour zone.

Then, one night hurrying home from a late

meeting at church, I saw the flashing blue light of a patrol car at the foot of the hill. *Good enough,* I mused. *The only way speeders are going to learn is if they get stopped and have to pay the penalty for their negligence.*

I automatically braked down the hill, passed the patrol car, and eased to a stop at the intersection. I couldn't resist glancing in my rear view mirror to spy on the scenario I imagined—the patrolman writing out a ticket and making his point about safe driving to some speeder. Instead, I saw the flashing blue light advancing behind *my* car, edging *me* off onto the shoulder.

Wonder if my taillight is burned out, I thought as I rolled down my window, ready to hear about my car's problem. The problem, I soon discovered, was not with my car, but with me.

"In a hurry?" queried the young officer. "My partner's up at the straight stretch where twenty-five-miles-an-hour is posted and his radar clocked you at thirty-eight. By the time you reached me you were at thirty-two."

"Me?" I answered incredulously. "I'm just on my way home from church." My face flushed at my self-righteous dodge.

"Driver's license, please." The officer was all business. He took my license, strode back to his car, and checked my driving record and our car license on his computer.

Five minutes passed, but it seemed like fifteen. My thoughts began racing to my defense. *He's young enough to be my son. I wonder if this is his first week out, and he's overzealous to bring in some kind of quota on traffic tickets.* I waited with my eyes glued to my rear view mirror, consoling myself that my good driving record would get me off with a warning this time.

Returning to my window, the officer handed back my license. "Did you know that two teenagers were killed on this road a few months ago?"

"Yes. Our son was on the track team with them. It was a terrible loss."

"We're concerned about saving lives on this stretch and we're not compromising our standards, even for good drivers. You have a choice of either mailing in a check for fifty-seven dollars or going before the judge if you want to protest it."

Two weeks later I drove to the district court for my late afternoon hearing with the judge.

"Well, well, caught going down the old treacherous turn, eh?" The judge in his early fifties was kindly and relaxed. "Your address tells me that you live in the neighborhood. Probably just slipped this time. However, one slip could be just as fatal as those of the habitual speeder."

He was right and I knew it. My flimsy rationalization didn't excuse me; I was guilty. I reached for my checkbook, but the judge intervened.

"We're determined to whip this area into a safe stretch by enforcing the law there. I can't compromise that decision. The only thing I can do is give you something you don't deserve—I'll drop the fine in half." He looked me directly in the eye and added, "Let's just call it *mercy*."

Mercy? I couldn't believe it! In the judge's chambers of that little district traffic court where I deserved punishment, I was given mercy. The proud, self-righteous one, guilty of breaking the law, had met up with an honest judge who wouldn't compromise his high standards of justice. Yet he had given compassion to the undeserving offender.

As I drove home that day, I remembered anew that justice and mercy comprise the heart of the Gospel. A just and merciful God has reached down to save us, and paid for all our slips, foibles, mistakes, and sins through Jesus' blood. We don't have to spend time in flimsy rationalization.

This Easter, let's share that same life-changing Gospel in the power of the Holy Spirit. In a world riddled with "treacherous turns" and "harrowing hills" it's our only hope.

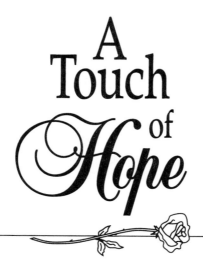

CHAPTER TEN

A Touch of Hope

"For I know the plans I have for you,"
declares the Lord, "plans to prosper you
and not to harm you, plans to give you
hope and a future."

Jeremiah 29:11

Rx for Sinking Spells

*O*ne day last week I crumpled. Caved in. Folded my tent. Without a doubt, I had a full-blown case of "the staggers." You wouldn't have missed it if you'd seen me drive home from work on "limp," drag myself through the front door, and drop into the sagging director's chair in the kitchen.

"Enough, world," I said as I leaned over to bump the phone off its hook. I let out a granddaddy sigh, then switched to groan as I heard the evening paper hit our front porch. And instead of bringing it in, I just kicked off my shoes and growled at our springer spaniel. *Well, why not? I thought. In this dog-eat-dog world, we deserve a little role reversal once in awhile.*

Stunned, Wendy slunk outside and quickly passed along the word to our cats, Felix and Ursula: *Beware, baaad mood inside.*

At our house, we've always called such downers "sinking spells." These are times when you feel that life has wrestled you to the mat or that you've just pushed the down button of your personal elevator and expressed yourself to the sub-basement. Paraphrasing the words of the poet Wordsworth, "The world is too much with you."

Usually, at least for me, what we're really talking about is perspective—losing it—and then wallowing in its void.

It's rarely the big crises that steal our vision; more often it's little things piling up that fuel a "sinking spell." The Bible calls them "the little foxes that ruin a vineyard."

That day last week, I could almost hear those little foxes barking. An ugly tale of child abuse spilled out on the morning news; a friend called, anguishing over her mother's struggle with Alzheimer's disease; a college friend despaired for her alcoholic husband; another friend cried on the phone as she described the ridicule she'd gotten for refusing sex before marriage. Like a live target, I felt pain shooting from every quarter—physical, emotional, spiritual. Was there no end to it? I rallied to brew some tea, then sank again while the tea steeped. "Oh, God," I moaned, "there's too much pain in the world. I hurt."

Where do you go when you double over with that kind of pain? I wanted to put life on hold and escape to Shangri-la. Instead, I went upstairs; pulled on my jeans, sweatshirt, and tennis shoes; grabbed my garden gloves and pruning shears; and headed for the backyard.

The "little foxes" weren't barking outside. Or at least I couldn't hear them as I squared off against the blackberry vines invading our property. Forgetting all about the problems of the world, I yanked, pulled, and slashed at the entangled network of roots for two solid hours.

Then it surfaced—quietly, gently—perhaps like

the still, small voice Elijah heard. Unmistakable words: "Carol, it's okay to hurt."

Had I heard right? "It's okay to hurt"—the words delivered too much comfort to dismiss idly. For a few days I carried them around, mulling over their impact. And then a friend told me about her weekend with her ten-year-old son.

Grant, she'd felt, needed to see more of life than he was experiencing in the comfortable suburb where they lived. Mom took son in tow, and they spent a Sunday afternoon observing the street people.

For several hours they walked the streets, Grant stared at the people in food lines, witnessed the despair in their faces, noted their worn-out shoes, smelled the urine and garbage. To his surprise, these weren't faceless "bums" lying around drunk in the back alleys of the city. Unemployed and homeless, these were real people—young, middle-aged, and old. Families with little kids—cute little kids.

After awhile, Grant stopped talking. In fact, neither one spoke as they drove back to their suburb. Then, without warning, in the middle of the freeway, Grant's voice pierced the silence. "Mom," he wailed, "I can feel it coming." He gasped for breath and let the tidal wave hit. "It's *heartbrokenness*," he sobbed, giving vent as best he could to what his tender eyes and ears had taken in.

Heartbrokenness, sinking spell, whatever term we use, if you've experienced it, you know it; and what is more, you're in good company. In his book

Inside Out Larry Crabb describes this feeling as a "core sadness that will not go away—evidence of honest living in a sad world." Jesus knew this pain intimately.

According to Dr. Crabb, "No matter how richly we experience the Lord, we cannot avoid the impact of living in a fallen world as a fallen being. Neither could our Lord. In perfect communion with the Father, yet he was still a man of sorrows, gripped to the point of tears by the hardness of men's hearts."

We may never physically stand and weep over Jerusalem as Jesus did. But we can let our heartbrokenness, our sinking spells, drive us to face our pain for what it is—the sign of utter hopelessness apart from God. And then we can make another choice: to let that pain drive us passionately to his perspective—and to his arms.

Antidote for the "Overwhelms"

eter, Jacob, Gretchen, and Frieda. Four little basket-carrying Dutch kids. Remember them from your childhood reading? Innocence bundled in excitement, they were out for a day gathering nuts in the country. A magnificent day. So successful, their baskets soon overflowed with their cache. Finally, toward evening, still exuberant, they skipped home under darkening skies.

All except Peter. The folk tale tells us that he spied water soaking into the sand along the dike and he stopped. "The water—the water from the sea is pouring through a hole in the dike." None of the other children felt Peter's urgency or perceived his worry. But he was adamant. He knew it was only a matter of time before the brewing storm would push the sea through the ever-widening hole and rush in to flood the land. As the rest scurried home in the descending twilight, Peter turned back to the dike.

We know the rest. The single-minded, brave little Dutch boy thrust his arm into the hole in the wall. All night he stayed, shivering and trembling as the bitter cold waters of the North Sea pummeled the dike with its human plug.

When morning comes, Peter is rescued, the dike repaired, and the flood averted. For a finale, a squad of soldiers carry the young hero home on their shoulders to his frantic mother.

I've thought of this little story lately when Christians tell me they feel overwhelmed. Tired. Stressed. Pulled on.

Fearful of living in the world of the nineties. Weary of coping in a society where the pace of living is accelerating in staggering dimensions.

Know the feeling? I do. You're coasting along in your own little world, listening to praise tapes in your car, reading the Bible through in a year, praying for your kids, picking up litter on the sidewalks—doing the "good Christian" things and then, out of the blue, the "overwhelms" catch you off guard. Like an attack dog, they go for the throat.

Child abuse, drugs, terrorists' killings—the news bombards you and emotionally wrestles you to the ground. When you stagger to your feet, you feel clobbered. Here you were, minding your own business, when some kind of cosmic garbage truck stops at your place—and dumps. The onslaught hits; the world is not only spinning too fast, it is not user friendly. Evil seems rampant—and mutating.

When the "overwhelms" hit, my first reaction is to run. And the second is like Peter's—I'll thrust myself against this onslaught. I'll plug the hole so the dike won't break. Urgency can be a clever distorter; and, in its grip, I forget who's responsible for this planet and its people. From there I spiral downward.

Are there antidotes for this kind of poisonous thinking? Yes! At a recent family dinner our kids reminded me of one: laughter. Time and again it has gotten our family back on track. Laughter. Unbridled, spontaneous, belly-level, roll-on-the-floor laughter.

"Remember the trip to Yellowstone?" The four of them—now all young adults—posed the question in unison as they sat reminiscing around our table, recalling the day laughter rescued the whole family.

Picture the scene: The perfect American family returning home from a two-week "dream" vacation—exploring a national park. Four kids packed into a station wagon with sleeping bags, suitcases, and the ice chest. Never forget the ice chest. We used it to separate two girls who were mortally pinching each other.

Everyone was tired. I'd thrown my back out. Dick was worn down with justifying why "every school child should see and *appreciate* his country." In cryptic language, the kids took turns expressing why they wished they'd been born in another family, one that toured Hawaii or Disneyland.

We felt like the American Gothic couple. Silent and uptight. The kids were fighting, and we were mad. We hurtled past the Craters of the Moon in southern Idaho with nary a mention of its geological uniqueness. We exchanged a silent, grim, knowing message: our car was full of "ungrateful beasties."

Then I sneezed—loud enough to wake the dead. A snicker arose from a kid in the second seat. I started giggling. Timidly. Then real laughter erupted and spread like brushfire. We were all laughing our heads off. Dick pulled into a rest stop and the six of us piled out, trying to walk while bent over in hysterical laughter. We went in our respective restrooms laughing and we emerged still laughing.

Onlookers shook their heads. One man made an aside to his wife: "Weird family." She responded, "Catch the license plate." That set us off for another ten miles of hilarious, unrestrained laughter. And then, a new perspective. Relief. Peace. And even love again.

Long before Norman Cousins laughed himself back to health by watching funny movies or anyone ever heard of laughter releasing healing endorphins, the Bible advocated it. Ecclesiastes reminds us of a *"season for every activity under heaven...a time to weep and a time to laugh"* (Eccles. 3:1,4).

The Holy Spirit is well able to show us how to "plug the holes" when the tide of evil pounds against the dikes around us. But oh, how we need to take our God more seriously and ourselves less so. And Christians, we, of all people, can afford to laugh. Not at the tragedy of sin. But because God is still in charge and has the final word, we need to laugh—even in the midst of the "overwhelms."

Penetrate the Darkness

$\mathcal{W}$e're heading for the island!" The kids
could hardly contain their excitement. It
was an Easter week vacation several years back,
and a friend and I decided to combine our broods
and take our collective eight children for a few
days' break in the San Juan Islands, north of Seattle.

Our husbands, whose schedules were busiest in
mid-April, commended us for our bravery and
promised us their prayers.

So two aging station wagons, loaded down
with sleeping bags, groceries, games, and two
moms with four kids each, drove on to the super
ferry at Anacortes for the trip through the beautiful
San Juan archipelago to Orcas Island.

Our stay was filled with simple fun: beach-
combing, excursions in the rowboat out to
Freeman's Island, trips to town to the craft shop
during rainstorms, games, a few minor sibling
squabbles, and the ritual evening marshmallow
roasts.

On our last night the youngest in our group,
Kristi, got sick. Nothing serious—just a flu bug or a
mild overdose of goodies. But since the upset came
at 10:30 P.M., I volunteered to fetch the clean linens
while her mother comforted her. Off I went to the
manager's office for fresh towels and sheets. No

heroic errand on my part, just a ten-minute stroll down the tree-lined road. In a flash I arrived, and, mission fulfilled, I began my trek back. I was about a quarter of the way back to our cabin when, without warning, the large vapor light illuminating the road clicked off.

After my initial surprise, my first thought was how really dark darkness is. The thick branches of the towering Douglas firs and a moonless, cloudy sky formed a veritable black blanket over that road. While I was certainly in no danger of falling into the water or off a precipice, it was simply too dark to see anything, much less where I was going.

I cannot see a thing. This is ridiculous. Why didn't I bring a flashlight? More amused than anxious, I got down on my knees; crawling was the only way I could navigate back to the cabin. The whole predicament struck me funny, and I giggled as I inched along a few feet at a time. I'd reach my destination. Sure, I'd have dirt-covered jeans and a few fir needles on my hands, but I'd make it. I had only one immediate problem: I couldn't see where I was going.

I recalled times when as a hiker, I'd needed an extra sweater or another sandwich. But I needed neither clothing nor food now. My problem was the darkness, and my need was for light. A flashlight or even a lighted match would have helped. I'd even have settled for taking the hand of someone who could have led me safely through the dark.

Once securely back at the cabin I gave little

thought to "how dark dark is" and my great need for a light again. Then nearly a year later, while I was reading the Sermon on the Mount in Matthew, it all came back.

In this scripture, you remember, Jesus tells us, *"You are the light of the world. A city on a hill cannot be hidden. Neither do people light a lamp and put it under a bowl. Instead they put it on its stand, and it gives light to everyone in the house. In the same way, let your light shine"* (Matt. 5:14).

Like instant replay I was back crawling along that Orcas Island dirt road, groping with the impenetrable darkness. This time I didn't giggle. I was confronted by the truth of Jesus' simple commission.

"Penetrate the darkness," Jesus seemed to say. "As a candle is lit by fire, so your life is ignited by mine. (*'In him was life, and that life was the light of men'* [John 1:4]). That light has the capacity to pierce darkness, dispel shadows, expose evil—all to resist the work of the usurper." Jesus knew that the only power in the universe capable of transforming darkness into light is God's life.

As his lightbearers we are called to be determined, committed people who fight passivity and hand-wringing in our encounters with the wicked forces of darkness—forces that breed havoc in our homes, churches, and nations. Like the virtuous woman of Proverbs 31, we are challenged to *"get up while it is still dark"* and not to let our candle go out *at night*, to pray, to intercede, to perservere in works of kindness initiated by the Holy Spirit, to lay down our lives for others in the midst of what appears to be the very darkest and most hopeless of hours.

Dark is dark, I learned while crawling on that dirt road, clutching sheets and towels. God, however, is more concerned with our acknowledging his ultimate purpose rather than our analyzing the darkness. He urges us to take action, based on the truth of his Word. *"Arise, shine, for your light has come, and the glory of the Lord rises upon you"* (Isa. 60:1). In the midst of a crooked and depraved generation, we are to shine as stars in the universe, holding out the word of life (Phil. 2:15) with the full knowledge that his light shines in darkness and the darkness has never overcome it (John 1:5).

CHAPTER ELEVEN

A Touch at *Christmas*

*Arise, shine, for your light has come,
and the glory of the Lord rises upon you.*
Isaiah 60:1

The Length of Love

his year Dick and I decided to celebrate our wedding anniversary at the ocean. Unusual for us because we're so attached to Puget Sound, where we live. Its inlets, its gentle tides, its extraordinary sea life, and its rocky beaches surrounded by evergreen trees have satisfied us over the years in ways that defy explanation. However, we yearned to see the Pacific Ocean, to be awed by a force bigger than ourselves.

And we were not disappointed. We walked along the shore in front of the lodge where we stayed. The pounding surf thundered against the sandy beach, loud, unrelenting, magnificent but at the same time frightening. Both of us made a stab at describing how we felt, but finally we simply stopped talking. All the usual adjectives stuck in our throats. Dwarfed by power and majesty, we were silenced by the ocean's grandeur and our insignificance.

We ate dinner that night at a little pizza place a few blocks back from the crashing waves. "I'm not sure I can cope with just sticking around the ocean," Dick volunteered. "How about heading inland tomorrow? Maybe explore some of the bays and villages on the other side of the peninsula?"

"You've got my vote, Honey," I assured him.

165

"I'm feeling intimidated by all that water. Out of my comfort zone against such bigness. I think I'll have to take the ocean in small doses."

That's how we happened to stumble upon the little village of Nahcotta along Willapa Bay. Little more than a wide spot in the road, Nahcotta was in the throes of its biggest event of the year—a garlic festival. We couldn't believe our eyes. Hordes of people, locals and tourists, descended on a narrow strip of road where dozens of booths blatantly extolled the marvels of garlic.

There were garlic bouquets, garlic presses, garlic wreaths, garlic cookbooks, as well as every imaginable culinary goody—soup, salad, pasta, and bread. Dick and I capitulated to the enticing aroma of Hungarian sausage soup. Then, foolishly, we capped off our lunch with a frosted raspberry torte, never dreaming it too was laced with garlic.

But the piece de resistance wasn't among all the garlic-laden food. Instead it was in the afternoon's major attraction: an outdoor garlic wedding. We had no idea this was an annual event, one where more than seven hundred couples had applied to be married. And here we were, celebrating our twenty-ninth anniversary and finding ourselves unintentionally among the wedding guests.

The milling crowed squeezed us into the front row, next to the arch where the bride and groom would exchange their vows. Talk about a switch from the day before! From two insignificant beach walkers we'd just been upgraded to honored guest status; we were shoved up against the TV crews and photojounalists who'd driven all the way from Seattle to report the garlic wedding.

Enter bridal attendants: two women dressed as garlic cloves in puffy green and white pads, with white tights and pink slippers. They were followed down the aisle by another woman dressed like an oversized crab, complete with orange shell and pinchers.

As the marimba and the bongo drums played under the canopy behind the arch, the groom, his best man, and the black-gowned judge slipped under the ropes and took their places facing the crowd.

Dick nudged me, "Look to your right, or you'll miss the bride." I didn't want to miss anything, although I admit my curiosity was edging toward skepticism.

Enter the bride and maid of honor. Dressed in gray tuxes, they were seated on top of a white convertible that quietly nosed its way through the crowd and stopped short of the lattice arch. They hopped off and strolled down the gravel aisle.

The judge made a few opening remarks to the crowd and the ceremony began. I'd never witnessed a civil ceremony before. The carnival-type atmosphere suddenly felt empty, hollow, and bleak. "Something's missing," I whispered to Dick.

"You mean *Someone*, he whispered back.

The judge asked the bride and groom to repeat their vows after him: "For better, for worse; for richer, for poorer; in sickness and in health." He paused. Then he delivered the clincher: "As long as love lasts."

"As long as love lasts!" The words hit us like cold water in the face.

How long does human love last? What is the length of it? Dick and I couldn't speak for the garlic couple, yet we knew from our own experience that our love was at times stretched, strained, and battered until it was threadbare under the stress of daily living. Job pressures, financial strains, time demands with four kids, not to mention our own penchant for selfishness, all extracted from love's store. There were times when we felt like we'd "given at the office" or at home all day and no love was left.

When Jesus comes to weddings, miracles have been known to happen. Had it not been that he took the water of our frail humanity in his hands and turned it into fine wine, we never would have known the secret of rich, staying love: *the Father's unconditional, everlasting love undergirding our own.*

At Christmas we look again at this kind of love and try to comprehend it in the infant Jesus. He's so unlike the awesome things that intimidate us— like pounding, crashing oceans. He is also unlike the world's hollow counterfeits. We can hardly take him in—absolute power and strength clothed in weakness, helplessness, and vulnerability—and destined to die for us.

How long does God's love last? Forever! What is the length of it? Measure it in Jesus!

Great Expectations

*T*he Lumpy Clam Chowder Story has become one of our family's favorite Christmas stories. While we usually prefer telling the *funny* reruns from past Christmases, the chowder story has, nevertheless, become a family classic. Over the years this tale continues to warm our hearts.

It happened on Christmas Eve ten years ago. Our house was fully decorated, fragrant with the scents we were accustomed to as part of our annual festivities—a mountain-fresh Douglas fir tree, pine boughs, a variety of food aromas lingering from the morning's baking, the fragrance of vanilla candles, and last, but not least, the smell of clam chowder simmering on the stove, the traditonal main dish for our light Christmas Eve supper.

I added the finishing touches to the chowder, fried bits of bacon and chopped parsley. *Hmm, smells pretty good,* I thought. *Almost ready to serve.* The phone rang. Within ten minutes I'd received three phone calls, all from people we'd invited to dinner the next day. For one reason or another, they were calling to cancel. They couldn't make it for Christmas dinner.

The last call was the most difficult for me. Dad, at the last minute, felt he just wasn't up to the six-hour drive across the snowy Cascade Mountains from his house to ours. Assuring us he'd miss us, he concluded our conversation with the promise he'd make it "next year for sure."

I was mildly annoyed. After all, we'd made a lot of special preparations with each of these people in mind. The kids had decorated place cards for everyone, and we'd even doubled the recipes on some of the salads "just for them."

Annoyance turned to irritation. This was really short notice to give a hostess—especially at Christmas time. Disappointment moved in fast.

I loved having the house filled with friends on Christmas. I had expected all these extra people to be with us, to enjoy the holiday together, to enhance our family celebration, and now, in ten minutes, my expectations had all been smashed.

Paul, our son who was ten at the time, came into the kitchen to check on the progress of supper and immediately ran headlong into the gloomy cloud hovering over my preparations. I stood at the stove staring into the chowder. Paul edged close to my side.

Without a word he handed me the wooden spoon. Not wanting to be critical, yet at the same time sensitive to my unfestive mood, he spoke hesitantly "Mom, lumps are in the chowder. And I don't think they're clams."

Sure enough, big lumps had formed while I'd been talking on the phone.

"Lumps could ruin the clam chowder, Mom." Wisdom, again, from a ten-year-old. "We've got to go after those lumps and rescue this soup."

The lumps in the chowder were nothing compared to the one in my throat. Yet Paul was suggesting we could turn things around, and, in my dark hour, I needed to hear that.

Things did turn around. That very night. First, we tackled the lumps in the clam chowder with the adept handling of two wooden spoons. Together, Paul and I attacked those big, white intruders and systematically squashed them, one by one.

Then I went to work on the lump in my throat.

That took more than the press of the wooden spoon. Some of my cherished ideas of what *had* to happen at Christmas—my misplaced expectations—needed to be "squashed" as vigorously as the lumps in the chowder.

When I made that choice, an idea came to mind. I would place three phone calls—one to a friend, one to my aunt, and one back to Dad. Each person, surprised by the unexpected Christmas Eve phone call, heard from me for the first time how deeply their love and kindnesses through the years had enriched my life. I reminded them of specific things they'd said or done. I heard the voices on the other end of the line warm with surprise and joy as I told them how much I cared about them.

Unbeknown to us then, all three of these precious people would not live to celebrate another Christmas on earth. Our young pastor friend, at twenty-six, died two weeks later of a ruptured aneurysm; my dad died of a heart attack; and my aunt, a stroke, both within six months.

We believe our Christmas Eve "turn-around" was the Lord's grace to us—a special gift that has changed every Christmas since. It started when we saw that a sturdy wooden spoon and some determination could salvage a lumpy chowder. Then we focused on the center of our Christmas celebration—Jesus, the babe of Bethlehem—the One who not only "saved the day" by giving grace to rout my disappointment and misplaced expectations, but who continues to "save us from ourselves" every day.

No circumstance can sidetrack the marvel of this gift. An unspeakable gift—the gift of Jesus, the Savior of the world and our Savior. Truly we can say, *"Our hope and expectation are from him"* (Ps. 62:5).

Hiccup in the Cathedral

*I*f you've visited the city of York in Northern England, you're not likely to forget its magnificent cathedral, the York Minster. When my husband and I stepped inside this enormous church—the largest Gothic cathedral in England—we instinctively stopped talking. And walking. For a few minutes we stood motionless in the nave, transfixed by the size and antiquity of this place.

As curious, excited tourists, we had no idea how dwarfed and insignificant we'd feel in this massive structure, and, at the same time, how captivated we'd be by its beauty. We finally "came to" and followed the guide to the altar where the late afternoon sun streamed through the medieval stained glass windows, splashed over our faces, and danced across our tennis shoes. Again, we were speechless.

Two years ago, we were back in York with two daughters and a friend. "You're on your own for seeing York," Dick announced, "except for one mandatory first stop—the Minster."

We arrived at the cathedral by 3:59 P.M., one minute before evensong began. The usher reluctantly raised the restraining rope and let the five of us in, cautioning us to tiptoe across the stone floor.

We eased into the front pew, directly across from where the visiting choir stood. I flinched when my camera bag clunked against the pew, and my purse slid to the floor. The woman on my right turned and frowned; the man behind me cleared his throat. I cringed at the obvious chastisement for irreverent tardiness.

The choir director raised his hands and in that infinitesimal moment before the first note sounded, the little girl next to me hiccupped—loudly. Then twice more—just as loudly.

"Mummy," she gasped, "I hiccuped." Her face was red. Mummy's face was redder. Everyone in that packed cathedral—the rector, the choir director, the choir, and the congregation heard the clear echo of a child's hiccup resonating through the infallible acoustics of a church built in 1220. But only our family heard her plaintive sob as she buried her head in her mother's shoulder: "Mummy, did I scare God away?"

Can you identify with her cry? I can. How often Satan has foisted that lie across our planet: that somehow our behavior—or even just our humanness—scares off a capricious God at the slightest provocation. Usually when we need him the most.

Once we buy that deception, we're ripe for the enemy's next ploy—to scare us into believing our worst fear: that we're really alone in this world after all.

If you're like me, at times in your life you've felt like an abandoned orphan, as if God were off hosting a party, but he'd forgotten to mail your invitation. You wondered if you'd "hiccuped" once too often, and he finally threw in the towel with you. After all, he'd put up with you long enough, and he had the cosmos to take care of.

No wonder we enjoy Christmas so much! What a perfect time to combat those lies with the truth— the truth that we have a God who runs *to* us, not *from* us—the truth about a loving Father who demonstrated his approachability two thousand years ago when he sent his love packaged in a helpless babe—the truth of Jesus who can be known by faith as One who rescues us, not abandons us.

Hearts are unusually open and soft at Christmas. It can be a wonderful time for renewal—for ourselves and for those around us. A time to retell the arsenal of stories from the Bible (and from experiences) that remind us again that God is always with us.

Remember Simeon? He was a mere "bit-player" in the nativity drama, but we can relate to him as we think of his soul's longing to see the promised Messiah. God finally gave him "hands-on" knowledge of the Lord. Simeon took the infant Jesus in his arms and declared, *"My eyes have seen your salvation, which you have prepared in the sight of all people"* (Luke 2:30,31).

And Anna, the prophetess. She prayed and fasted in the temple every day. At age eighty-four, she saw the answer to her prayers as she witnessed Simeon's blessing on Jesus, the Hope of Israel. She knew God's promise was true. Both saints lived to see the evidence that God does not leave his people. They saw Emmanuel!

A dear retired Estonian pastor friend of ours tells of his most memorable Christmas—when the Lord made himself known in the barracks of a freezing Siberian prison camp during World War II. The men had secretly dragged in a tiny fir tree from the woods where they labored ten hours a day. They decorated it with scraps of paper and medicine vials saved to fill with heating oil. When they lit the oil and sang a Christmas hymn, those weary men, stripped of home, family, and traditions, experienced the presence of their Savior. Jesus was with them, strengthening their weak bodies and encouraging their spirits.

In her book *Life and Death in Shanghai*, Nien Cheng, a courageous Chinese woman imprisoned for seven years during the Cultural Revolution, describes a Christmas Eve in her cramped, dank cell. Physically and emotionally depleted from hours of interrogation and abuse and engulfed in aloneness, she suddenly heard the Father speak. From two cells down, a lovely lyric soprano voice dared to penetrate that evil atmosphere with "Silent Night"—on pitch and in perfect Chinese. Emmanuel was with her!

At Christmas, we're tempted to rail against those things that appear to keep the Lord at a distance—the noisy malls, the blatant commercialism, the selfish materialism, all our "'hiccups' in the cathedrals." How much better to do what the angels did when Jesus came close in Bethlehem: Focus on the truth, believe the truth, and sing it out for all the world to hear—"Glory to God in the highest."

Walking for Life

I recently read something in a national newsmagazine that confirmed one of my cherished contentions: a daily walk makes a difference in one's marriage. I knew it! I'd never seen it in print before, but there between a foreign-policy report and an economic forecast was a full-page article extolling the merits of a nightly stroll with one's spouse.

I was impressed. Not just because of my prejudice for walking, but because the author had done his homework. Although he advised against trying to repair a troubled marriage with "just a walk," he encouraged his readers with statistical evidence of the benefits couples derive from walking.

Dick and I talked about the article and left it on the coffee table where sixteen-year-old Jane later picked it up and read it. "I don't get it," she quipped. "Why's walking such a big deal?" It took awhile, but she did get her answer.

Ten years ago when Dick and I first began walking through the neighborhood, our motives were simple: we needed exercise, and Jenny, our big yellow lab, needed a nightly workout. However, as our four children became teenagers our reasons changed.

We needed grace and time alone, counting on

the walk as a precious forty-five-minute respite from answering homework questions and negotiating TV time. Then gradually—imperceptibly—we felt the benefits accumulate.

We discovered we could sort through a disagreement or wrestle with a financial decision as we padded through the neighborhood. We could rhapsodize about the neighbors' flowers or their Christmas decorations. Or we didn't have to talk at all; we could just watch the sun sink behind the Olympic Mountains or let the winter rain drizzle across our faces. By the time we returned, the dog would be too tired to bark at the moon, but we'd be rejuvenated—physically by the exercise, emotionally and spiritually by our just walking quietly together.

In recent years, we've walked beyond the neighborhood. Needing more exercise for ourselves and for Wendy, our rambunctious springer spaniel, we now walk the three miles around Seattle's Green Lake once or twice a week.

Last Saturday daughter Gail joined us as we headed out before dusk. A newspaper reporter, Gail thrives on adventure. As usual she had a proposal: "Let's keep track of all the walkers we pass and compare notes over a Coke on the way home. I'll walk Wendy, and you can pay for the Cokes." It was a deal.

So reversing directions, we faced the walkers head on, intent on tallying the great diversity of the human race in fifty minutes.

Imagination in full gear, I started silently counting: Two sisters giggling about last night's slumber party. A hand-holding middle-aged couple. A thirty-year-old pushing his handicapped father in a wheelchair. Two turbaned men chatting amicably. A family of four—one baby in a backpack, a toddler in a stroller. A bearded man with a walking stick. Two joggers steaming by in their sweatsuits and headbands. A couple of career women analyzing their office personnel problems. And on and on until Coke time.

Our lists were different, yet as we tossed them around the table in the deli they were strikingly similar.

"It seems like more happens than just conversation when people walk together. There's closeness and intimacy."

"I sensed real communication—and a lot of listening."

"Almost everyone walked in step."

"Even those who walked by themselves didn't seem alone in the community of fellow walkers."

"Some couldn't have made it alone."

"Neither can we," Dick interjected. That was it! The clincher, the "big deal" about walking.

We were never meant to walk alone. Ever. Not on this earth. From the beginning God reached out to walk with Noah and his friend Abraham. All the while he kept telling his people, *"I will walk among you and be your God, and you will be my people"* (Lev. 26:12).

Commitment. God didn't draw back because of floods or giants or fiery furnaces or wars or scary places like the Valley of the Shadow. His promise never wavered, even when his people chose to walk with other gods, when they found it too hard to walk with a God they couldn't see. His promises and miracles weren't enough.

Finally, God came and walked with us in person. He came to a dusty hick town, not in kingly robes, but in the vulnerability of a helpless infant to begin his mission of getting us to our Father. Theologians call it the "incarnation," that wonderful miracle of God's coming to us in human form, to walk with us, to love, rescue and forgive us, to share his heart along the way even to the point of the cross.

And that's a "big deal." Walking with Jesus is, in fact, the *biggest* deal. No wonder the angels sang "Glory to God in the highest" when he came. They must have known we cannot make it walking alone.

Christmas Music

*N*either my husband nor I qualify as opera buffs. In fact, between us, we
haven't a trace of a musical gene. But two years
ago, we took a chance and spent a Sunday afternoon at the opera where, in spite of our musical
ignorance, we got hooked.

We couldn't believe it ourselves. When the arias
and the choruses exploded with romantic ecstasy
on one hand or soul-wrenching agony on the other,
the distance between us and the actors evaporated.
Their joy or pain became ours. It was heart-to-heart
stuff, like an emotional aerobic workout set to clas-
sical music. Even as novices, we knew we wanted
more.

So when *Madame Butterfly* came to town last
month, Dick and I went. In our naivete, we never
realized this opera was one of the emotional
"biggies," although we should have suspected it
when several friends warned us to take handker-
chiefs.

We should have had a clue when we read the
director's words in the program: "Everyone relates
to betrayal..." Nevertheless, no warning could have
prepared us for the final scene.

Butterfly, a Japanese geisha, has waited three
long years for her American naval-lieutenant hus-

band to come back to her "when the robins nest again," as he promised. Her confidence in his return is unswerving, although others see that for Pinkerton the marriage was only a passionate fling, a "sham marriage." Gently, they try to persuade her to give up believing he'll return.

Her faith in Pinkerton, however, is unshakable, and she tells us so in the incredibly beautiful aria, "Some Day He'll Come."

Finally, his ship sails into the harbor. Pinkerton has returned to Japan. But he's not come for Butterfly, and he's not come alone. He's brought his American bride with him—to take his and Butterfly's little son back with them.

Betrayal. The sting flies tangibly to the audience. Butterfly gave her heart to Pinkerton. In return, he betrayed her. Devastated. Distraught. With nothing now to live for, she takes her life.

Silence. Stunned silence. Betrayal's impact swept over the audience in one crushing wave. I reached for my handkerchief. Dick reached for his. All around us in the big Seattle Opera house, people were sniffling and blowing. The woman next to me doubled over in full-blown sobs.

A red-eyed crowd stood for the curtain call, clapping wildly. Butterfly swept low in her final bow, and the audience, from the main floor to the second balcony, threw off all restraints and let go: "Bravo, bravo, bravo." These weren't just the shouts of music critics or opera buffs enraptured with an outstanding soprano voice. These were cries from people whose hearts ached for Butterfly.

They identified with the pain of her rejection.

Then came Pinkerton's turn. No one could deny the tenor's powerful voice and skillful acting. But objectivity faded fast in that charged atmosphere. To divorce his performance from his role as betrayer was impossible. Not only did the applause lessen, a few unbridled boo's shot out from the audience.

Like the program said, "Everyone relates to betrayal." We experience it even before we learn the word. Our parents sneak out the backdoor, leaving us with a baby-sitter, and our little hearts scream in terror. The next time that baby-sitter comes, our guard is up. The first brick of a self-protective wall falls into place.

The girlfriend who promised to keep our deepest secret, doesn't; it gets back to us. We overhear teachers laugh in the lunchroom about our "stupid" answer in class. Our parents get a divorce. The betrayal syndrome cranks into motion; brick by brick, the wall grows higher.

If left unchecked, the progression is insidious. By adulthood, when we think the world should finally quit handing us betrayal on a silver platter, we find instead we're in the "big-time." Our precious kids turn on us and call us failures; our bosses give the promotion to someone else; the church hurts us; then, to some, the worst of all pain—our spouse leaves us for someone else.

No wonder people in the opera house cried— and booed. Show us betrayal, and we relate. We want to rescue poor Butterfly, kill the villain, and commend ourselves for staying inside our own little protective walls where we feel safe. We want to do anything but admit that the real culprit is not the villain outside us, but our own choice to hold back our heart from the One who made it. Instead of getting free, we set ourselves up for more betrayal.

"Some Day He'll Come." Butterfly's song reminds us of the Old Testament prophets' message, the word of hope preached to skeptical, stubborn, hurting hearts. The Messiah, a savior/lover, will come.

The incredible Christmas news is that Jesus will not betray us. He is no Pinkerton. He *will* rescue us with his unfailing love, take our heart in his hands, and fill it to overflowing.

This Christmas, give Jesus your heart—again. And again. And again. Then listen carefully. You'll hear the sound of bricks falling from your wall of protection. And that's Christmas music!

The Gift that Lasts

I still remember my favorite Christmas gift, Nancy Anne, a doll with real hair. She arrived under the Christmas tree wearing a green sweater handknit by my Danish grandmother, a green taffeta dress, and white buckle shoes. Marvel upon marvels, Nancy Anne's bright eyes blinked open and shut when I moved her head. (This was long before battery implants enabled dolls to walk and talk to their young mothers.) Her silky-soft red hair was incredibly pliable and invited my seven-year-old fingers to braid and curl it for hours at a time, despite the adults' warning that it wouldn't last if I continued to do so.

The adults, it turned out, were right. Nancy Anne's hair didn't last very long, and neither did she. Literally loved to pieces, she eventually was replaced by other dolls.

This side of Heaven, it seems, our gifts don't last forever; even those that delight us the most have a limited life span and their ability to affect our lives is, at best, temporary.

This Christmas, however, I'm recalling another gift, one I received fifteen years ago, which will forever impact my life. Because of this gift, my "head" knowledge of the Gospel was pushed a lot closer to "heart" knowledge. Ever since that event,

I've *known* that the Gospel really is God's Good News to this world.

My remarkable gift was a young woman named Dixie. She was, I'm certain, God-sent. Who else but God could have orchestrated such incredible, extravagant love by frustrating the hopelessness of a terminal illness, and, at the same time, use Dixie to make a timid Christian bold in proclaiming the Gospel? Who else could have graphically illustrated the power of forgiveness to transform a life?

Dixie was an out-of-town cancer patient needing local visitors to fill in for distant friends and family. My intentions were noble enough, but I was woefully ignorant of how to communicate with a dying person, let alone share the love of Jesus on a personal basis.

By the time I met Dixie she weighed about ninety-five pounds; the disease had advanced rapidly, and her physical vitality was nearly depleted. Yet her mind was razor sharp. I can still hear her gravelly voice verbally pinning me to the hospital wall as she tried to get her do-good visitor to answer her questions about God.

"How come you're bothering with me? You've probably got a lot of better things to do than waste your time visiting a cancer patient you don't even know. What happened—did your church run out of things to do and needed another project?"

Dixie's rapid-fire barrage caught me up short. I was disarmed. She was a *person*, not a *project*, and after her initial monologue I never forgot that distinction.

"Well, I *am* from a church," I managed. "And I'd just like to spend some time with you since you're so far from your home. "

"From a church, huh? So what do you have to offer? I could use some good news about now."

Startled by her abruptness, I plunged ahead. "We like to reach out, to help people." But as I looked at Dixie, little more than skin and bones, her dark eyes mirroring her hopelessness, my words suddenly sounded trite and hollow. "We try our best to give people a hand, like take over a casserole or baby-sit in emergencies. It's part of the Gospel, you know, to show God's love..."

As weak as she was Dixie pulled herself up in bed, leaned on one elbow and challenged me. "I obviously don't need a casserole or a baby-sitter. What I need to know is whether or not God will forgive this old milltown prostitute and show up and love me before I die. Don't give me a part of the Gospel, either; it's all good news or it's nothing."

She lay back, only to add her final "zinger." "Unless you've got the guts to tell it straight, don't waste your time."

I struggled with that all night. I had never learned to evangelize. But Dixie didn't have time to wait for me to learn how—she needed the Gospel now.

The next morning I strode resolutely into Room 203. Dixie lay curled in a fetal position, breathing heavily. I took hold of her thin hand and spelled out the Gospel like I'd never done before. "Jesus loves you, Dixie. He died to save you from your sins. He wants you to receive his gift of life."

A few questions later, and, miracle or miracles, Dixie looked me in the eye and said softly, "That's good news. I believe it."

The Gospel took root, and, in Dixie's remaining days, I saw a spiritual revolution. From bitterness to peace. From guilt to forgiveness. From anger to joy. From death to life.

God's gift to Dixie was eternal salvation. His gift to me was Dixie. From her I learned what Paul meant when he wrote, *"I am not ashamed of the gospel, because it is the power of God for the salvation of everyone who believes"* (Rom. 1:16).

Now that's a Christmas gift that lasts.

CHAPTER TWELVE

A Touch at Easter

I know that my Redeemer lives...
Job 19:25

Man on the Loose

*W*e were all freezing. Ten of us in our adult class. We shivered together and blew icy puffs into the frosty air of our church fireside room. After a week of sixty-degree days, we weren't prepared for the thirty-degree temperature drop. Nor was the janitor who'd neglected to turn up the heat.

March can be a topsy-turvy, yo-yo month in the Pacific Northwest. Spring saunters in unannounced, and then just as we shelve our scarves and gloves, winter barges back in, determined to clutch us a little longer.

This particular morning, however, we were rescued from complaining about the weather by the sounds of coffee perking on the sideboard and logs crackling in the fireplace. Our disappointment assuaged by the prospects of immediate human comforts, we settled in for our assault on Romans 6.

Then just as we started grappling with Paul's explanation of law and grace, the door swung open and in stormed a dirty, disheveled young man. Dressed in heavy trousers and layers of ragged sweaters topped with a rumpled overcoat, he stalked past our table and plunked down on the sofa facing the fireplace.

He cleared his throat. We turned and stared. He

191

rubbed his red hands. We looked at each other wondering: *Who is this guy?*

He plopped two logs on the fire and headed for the coffee. We swiveled in our chairs, following his actions. My husband, leader of the study, finally broke the silence. "Would you like a cup of coffee?"

"Yup."

"You're welcome to pull up a chair and join our Bible class," Dick continued.

Another one-word answer: "Nope."

I remembered the food left over from our packing boxes for the food bank and knew we could make him breakfast on the spot. "How about some toast and fruit juice to go with your coffee?"

"No." His answer was pointed. No more offers.

We resumed our class. I watched this stranger out of the corner of my eye. He didn't stay seated long; he strolled over to the piano and played a couple of scales. Then, bowing to his imaginary audience, he returned to the fireplace, positioned himself cross-legged, and began blowing on the fire.

I had difficulty concentrating on Romans 6. Questions cascaded through my mind. *Can we help this guy? Why are his eyes so wild-looking? Is he on drugs? Should we usher him out?*

Ambivalent feelings. I had a good case of them. Someone had stumbled into the Lord's house on his day, and here we were reading his Word, torn between compassion and fear, wanting to reach out, but scared of this wild man. I felt uncomfortable.

As we were winding up the class, our intruder-friend abrupty left the room. He headed into the sanctuary where the eleven o'clock service was beginning. I saw him pen a note and place it on the lectern. Apparently satisfied his note would be read, he sat in the front pew, only to hop up and play another scale on the piano.

By this time the congregation was aware of the stranger's presence. Whispering was rampant. A couple of people, uneasy with the smell and unpredictable behavior of the man, moved across the aisle. Ushers were poised to pounce if necessary, yet uncertain what to do. Our pastor gave the announcements, but he ignored the note, a demand, we learned later, for a million dollars.

Finally in the middle of the sermon, our unknown friend stood to his feet, strode down the side aisle and outside to the chilly March morning. Gone from our midst.

We talked about it after church. Could we have helped him? Should we have called the police or the drug rehab center down the street? The consensus was that we'd better think of some strategies for next time. After all, what would we do if a mad man *really* got loose in our church? Imagine!

Then I remembered another Man on the loose, a Man in first century Palestine. He wasn't mad or even potentially dangerous like our Sunday morning stranger may have been, although some claimed he was. He, too, burst upon the scene, upset the status quo, and did what no one before had ever done, especially in "religious" circles. Wild, unpredictable, scandalous things.

Outrageous things. Things like forgiving undeserving people and accepting sinners even before they repented. Things like welcoming home dirty, wayward kids or healing people with tainted pasts. Things like talking to women as equals and eating supper with cheaters. Extravagant things like loving us as we are instead of as we ought to be. And finally dying to pay the price of all our rebellion.

But the Easter news tells us that this Someone still lives. Jesus, God's Man, lives! Oh, what would happen if we dared loose him—in our private worlds, our homes, our churches?

Closing the Gap

"H ey, Lady, you gonna go to heaven?" The question shot out of nowhere, and I ignored it. But like radar tracking, it honed in on its target. "Yeah, *you*, lady." No doubt about it, the young man leaning against the airport concourse wall was questioning me.

I slipped my carry-on bag and purse onto the conveyor belt of the metal detector, turned, and called back my answer: "You bet I'm going to heaven." End of conversation and on to the boarding gate where those headed for New Orleans were talking animatedly. In all the excitement, no one mentioned being questioned by the twentyish-looking guy who'd apparently quizzed others about their eternal destiny.

However, later, as I walked down the jetway, I overheard the passengers behind me laughing about a "religious nut" who'd polled them about their ticket to heaven. I smiled smugly as I handed my ticket to the flight attendant, mentally replaying the earlier query as I stepped aboard: "Hey, lady, you gonna go to heaven?" I basked in my confident answer, my awareness of my salvation in Christ. It felt good to know the fear of death did not grip me.

Fearful? Not me. Nevertheless, I found myself paying close attention to the pre-flight emergency instructions. I turned my head to check the location of the nearest emergency exit. I even admitted to myself that I liked the overtones of competence and experience in the captain's voice when he introduced himself and sketched our route. Aloft, I relaxed, settling in for the ride to New Orleans, alternately reading *James Herriott's Dog Stories* and dozing as the plane headed south. This, indeed, was smooth sailing.

Smooth, that is, until an unexpected bounce jolted me awake. The seat belt sign lit up, and simultaneously the captain reassured us: "We're experiencing a little turbulence. If it doesn't smooth out, we'll simply find a higher altitude. Meanwhile relax and keep your seat belts fastened."

The plane bounced along like a jeep over a washboard road. I didn't like it at all, but I diverted myself by leaning forward to peer out the window at the snow-capped Rockies below. I cinched in my seat belt; and as I did, my book slid off my lap to the floor. Bending over to retrieve it I noticed my hands; they were wet and sticky—in a word, clammy.

"You gonna go to heaven, lady?" The words echoed again, but this time my smugness was dissipating. My clammy hands were more honest than my thoughts. "Okay, Lord," I admitted, "I know I'm going to heaven. I'd just prefer not to go today."

Safe landings have a way of restoring perspective and objectivity, of allowing us another opportunity to view the gaps between what we believe in our head and what our hearts tell us. "Carol," I said later when I faced myself in the mirror, "you may be certain of heaven, but you're scared about getting there too soon. Where's your faith?"

That eighteen-inch gap between my head and my heart grabbed my attention. Familiar territory for this pilgrim. And I'm sure others have battled that same gap, that chasm separating what we want to believe and what our heart actually tells us. Who of us has not scrimmaged with it and come up gasping for help as reality poked holes in our pious pretentions?

Despite its many faces, "the gap" is easily recognizable. Like late-night TV reruns, the scenarios we experience are incredibly common. We're overlooked for a shower invitation and our head knows why—too many relatives to include—but our heart, because it has absorbed hurts and negative messages in the past, gives us another story: rejection. We think we believe that God loves us unconditionally; yet when we lose our temper at our kids, our heart condemns us with the indictment that we've just blown it: we've stepped over the line of God's grace and become unlovable.

How often I've bemoaned that gap. How often most of us have faced that distance between head knowledge and heart belief and felt we were looking across the Grand Canyon. Surely we ought to be more spiritually advanced than this! Why do we "lose it" so easily? Why do our wounded hearts continue to play havoc with our faith? And why do we then proceed to spiral down from exasperation to self-condemnation? What will ever close this gap?

The Lord never seems to take on my questions as a celestial high priority. I always hit a dead-end road when I plead for explanations.

Jesus, it seems, doesn't traffic in "why's" and "whatever's." Remember how he dismissed the disciples' question about the blind man in John 9? Assessing blame or analyzing faults wasn't his mission. He came to bring glory to his Father. He did it—and he continues to do it: healing and restoring broken, wounded hearts, rescuing us over and over—from ourselves, our doubts, and our fears.

Again I'm brought up short by Jesus, the good news of his death and resurrection, his offer of twenty-four-hour service with a prepaid price. It's the "Easter special" once more, where the empty tomb overrides our clammy-hand syndrome, and the grace of the victorious Christ reaches out to close those cavernous gaps inside.

"Hey, lady, you gonna go to heaven?"

"You bet. And I'm going first class. My ticket's stamped with the cross."

Outrageous Faith

"Where in the world did we get four bags of dried-up onions?" my husband asked as he walked through the utility room. "Unless you're planning to make onion soup for the whole neighborhood, I say, 'Let's toss these out.'"

"If you don't, I will," chimed daughter Jane. "Those dead things have been sitting around here for a month. Even the dog won't chew them."

That was last October, and I wasn't about to divulge the contents of the mystery bag then nor did I want the "onions" thrown out. I silenced them with the promise I'd take care of the matter myself.

Now as you read this five months later, the secret will soon be out, not only for Dick and Jane, but for our whole neighborhood and anyone else who passes by our street. Our house will be surrounded by the brightest yellow spectacle imaginable—one hundred giant Holland daffodils blooming their hybrid hearts out.

Through all the dark days of winter, I silently relished the moment when the first signs of my surprise would surface, when someone would spot the fresh green foliage pressing through the water-logged soil and demand to know what was happening in our hitherto barren flower beds. And even when I occasionally forgot about my secret "underground" project, another healthy rainstorm would remind me of that dreary October afternoon when a spunky, red-haired, nursery clerk challenged me to fight an attack of doubt with a visible statement of faith.

Torrential rains fell that day as I drove home from work. The racing window swipes barely cleared the windshield fast enough, and, even with headlights on, visibility was near zero. Inching along in the three o'clock traffic, I longed to be home by my fireplace, listening to good music, and enjoying a cup of tea.

I wasn't just battling the elements outside; I was also fighting a grief attack inside. Between the dreary weather and the pain of losing a close friend, my faith was at a low ebb. In fact, it crossed my mind that perhaps it was on a day like this that Job asked, "If a man dies, will he live again?"

I remembered that the sky was dark when Jesus cried out from the cross, "My God, my God, why have you forsaken me?"

I wondered what the day was like after the crucifixion when Peter, discouraged at the loss of his beloved master, said, "I'm going fishing."

Right in the middle of these thoughts, my eye caught a big red sign, barely visible through the rainstorm. "Sale—Giant Holland Bulbs—Plant Now."

Crazy. Foolish. Wild. But I did it anyway. I braked, made a quick left turn into the parking lot of the nursery, leapt from the car, and dashed through the drenching rain.

"A customer! I can't believe anyone would even get out of a car today," sang out the cheery, red-haired clerk. "This weather isn't fit for man or beast. The only thing that could bring anyone in today is either insanity or some kind of outrageous faith."

"I want one hundred Holland daffodil bulbs," I said.

"One hundred daffodils. Indeed, a woman of faith on a day like this." The clerk was ecstatic. She scooped up a handful of bulbs from the adjacent bin, plucking out one large one to hold up between us.

"Now I'd call this 'a miracle in the making.' Look at this scruffy thing—hardly more than a dried-up onion on its last legs. But, if you plant it six inches deep in loose soil, with a scattering of fertilizer and, if you're willing to wait five months, you're in for a burst of blinding color just when you've given up hope. With one hundred of these bulbs, my dear, your year's going to be singing 'Alleluia' next spring."

Had she somehow been privy to my thoughts of the last few hours? Or was she an angel in disguise? It didn't matter. Her words rang true, and they bulldozed my doubts.

I quietly gathered up the four big bags and headed home, eager for the first dry day to plant the bulbs. I was ready to make my statement of faith.

If a man dies, will he live again? "Yes!" shouts the Scriptures. Jesus' resurrection is historical fact.

God's Son died and lives again. If we don't believe this, says Paul, we are foolish, to be greatly pitied.

Will our God ever forsake us? "No!" shouts the Scriptures again. Jesus' death and resurrection has sealed our relationship with the Father and guaranteed our life with him forever.

Do we dare give up and just 'go fishing' like Peter during those dark days when we see no hope? No! Remember the resurrection of our Lord!

This Easter we'll be celebrating his resurrection with the help of one hundred blooming daffodils. And we'll be singing, "Alleluia." God has conquered death!

The red-haired clerk would call it "outrageous faith."